Planet Earth
RESTLESS OCEANS

This volume is one of a series that examines the
workings of the planet earth, from the geological
wonders of its continents to the marvels of its
atmosphere and its ocean depths.

Cover
A procession of waves, perhaps generated by
a gale hundreds of miles away, marches in from
the Pacific Ocean to break against the
western coast of the United States. Waves are
but one manifestation of the many ways in
which wind and water interact, with profound
effects for all life on the planet.

Planet Earth

RESTLESS OCEANS

By A. B. C. Whipple
and The Editors of Time-Life Books

Time-Life Books, Alexandria, Virginia

Time-Life Books Inc.
is a wholly owned subsidiary of

TIME INCORPORATED

FOUNDER: Henry R. Luce 1898-1967

Editor-in-Chief: Henry Anatole Grunwald
Chairman and Chief Executive Officer: J. Richard Munro
President and Chief Operating Officer: N. J. Nicholas Jr.
Chairman of the Executive Committee: Ralph P. Davidson
Corporate Editor: Ray Cave
Executive Vice President, Books: Kelso F. Sutton
Vice President, Books: George Artandi

TIME-LIFE BOOKS INC.

EDITOR: George Constable
Executive Editor: Ellen Phillips
Director of Design: Louis Klein
Director of Editorial Resources: Phyllis K. Wise
Editorial Board: Russell B. Adams Jr., Thomas H. Flaherty, Lee Hassig, Donia Ann Steele, Rosalind Stubenberg, Kit van Tulleken, Henry Woodhead
Director of Photography and Research: John Conrad Weiser

PRESIDENT: Christopher T. Linen
Chief Operating Officer: John M. Fahey Jr.
Senior Vice Presidents: James L. Mercer, Leopoldo Toralballa
Vice Presidents: Stephen L. Bair, Ralph J. Cuomo, Neal Goff, Stephen L. Goldstein, Juanita T. James, Hallett Johnson III, Robert H. Smith, Paul R. Stewart
Director of Production Services: Robert J. Passantino

PLANET EARTH

EDITOR: Thomas A. Lewis
Deputy Editor: Russell B. Adams Jr.
Designer: Albert Sherman
Chief Researcher: Patti H. Cass

Editorial Staff for *Restless Oceans*
Associate Editor: Marion F. Briggs (pictures)
Text Editors: Tim Appenzeller, Sarah Brash, Jan Leslie Cook
Researchers: Jane A. Martin, Judith W. Shanks (principals), Roxie M. France, Adrianne T. Goodman, John S. Marshall
Assistant Designers: Cynthia T. Richardson, Susan K. White
Copy Coordinators: Elizabeth Graham, Anthony K. Pordes
Picture Coordinator: Renée DeSandies
Editorial Assistant: Caroline A. Boubin

Special Contributor: Paul N. Mathless (text)

Editorial Operations
Copy Chief: Diane Ullius
Production: Celia Beattie
Quality Control: James J. Cox (director)
Library: Louise D. Forstall

Correspondents: Elisabeth Kraemer-Singh (Bonn); Maria Vincenza Aloisi (Paris); Ann Natanson (Rome). Valuable assistance was also provided by: Janny Hovinga, Wibo van de Linde (Amsterdam); Bob Gilmore (Auckland); Lois Lorimer (Copenhagen); Lance Keyworth (Helsinki); Peter Hawthorne (Johannesburg); Millicent Trowbridge (London); Cheryl Crooks (Los Angeles); John Dunn (Melbourne); Felix Rosenthal (Moscow); Christina Lieberman, Cornelis Verwaal (New York); Dag Christensen (Oslo); Ann Wise (Rome); Mary Johnson (Stockholm).

Library of Congress Cataloguing in Publication Data
Whipple, A. B. C. (Addison Beecher Colvin), 1918-
    Restless oceans.
    (Planet earth)
    Bibliography: p.
    Includes index.
    1. Ocean currents. 2. Marine pollution. I. Time-Life Books. II. Title. III. Series.
GC231.2.W48 1984   551.47'01   83-17909
ISBN 0-8094-4340-6
ISBN 0-8094-4341-4 (lib. bdg.)

THE AUTHOR

A. B. C. Whipple, a former Assistant Managing Editor of Time-Life Books, is the author of *Storm* in the Planet Earth series and of four volumes of the Seafarers library. Fifty years of sailing provided him with an informed appreciation of the behavior of ocean and tidal currents; further research for *Restless Oceans* took him from Scripps Institution of Oceanography in California to Woods Hole Oceanographic Institution in Massachusetts.

THE CONSULTANTS

Richard C. Vetter is a former Executive Secretary for the Board of Ocean Science and Policy at the National Academy of Sciences National Research Council. His responsibilities there included maintaining liaison between the governmental and private oceanographic communities by preparing and disseminating information about the progress of research. A founding member and fellow of the Marine Technology Society, he has coordinated, organized and participated in more than 50 workshops, seminars and meetings relating to all aspects of oceanography.

Dr. Eugene M. Rasmusson has seen three decades of service as a forecaster and researcher with the U.S. National Weather Service or its parent organization, the National Oceanic and Atmospheric Administration. His specialties include river and weather forecasting as well as research on the atmospheric water balance, the general circulation of the atmosphere, tropical meteorology and large-scale sea-air interaction. As Chief of the Diagnostic Branch of the Climate Analysis Center, Dr. Rasmusson closely followed the global climate anomalies associated with El Niño during 1983.

CONTENTS

A BRINY MANTLE FOR THE EARTH

The earth is misnamed, for it is more water than land. Seventy-two per cent of the planet is covered by a briny mantle whose depth averages two and a quarter miles. And, though geographers speak of many separate seas and oceans, the watery realm is not actually partitioned by land masses; it is a single ocean in which the continents are islands rather than barriers.

At either end, the globe is girdled by bodies of water — the Arctic Ocean beneath its perpetual cap of ice, and the Southern Ocean that surrounds Antarctica. Between these polar seas, like the prongs of Neptune's trident, the Indian, Pacific and Atlantic Oceans sprawl across the Equator.

Everywhere on earth the waters mingle and move in a three-dimensional structure that is staggering in its complexity. As one oceanographer has put it, "The ocean is motion." Storm winds scour the surface, whipping it into transient waves. Steadier, more constant winds drive the currents — vast, meandering rivers in the ocean that flow across its surface from season to season and year to year, accelerating or slowing but never disappearing. Beneath the undulating surface, masses of water rise and sink, propelled by variations in density and temperature. Because of the ocean's ceaseless circulation (slow though it can be — bottom water may take 2,000 years to creep to the surface), the chemical composition of sea water differs little from one part of the globe to another.

Ocean and atmosphere are engaged in a dynamic relationship. The winds that supply their energy to the ocean arise in part because of the huge quantities of heat the ocean absorbs from the sun, then transfers to the overlying air. Slow to warm and equally slow to cool, the moving waters transport heat thousands of miles from sunny equatorial regions to chill northern latitudes, moderating the climate and making the earth a far kinder habitat for all forms of life.

Spindrift whitens the crest of a breaking wave in the gale-driven Southern Ocean. The prevailing winds that constantly lash the waters near Antarctica drive a sea current that eternally circles the bottom of the world.

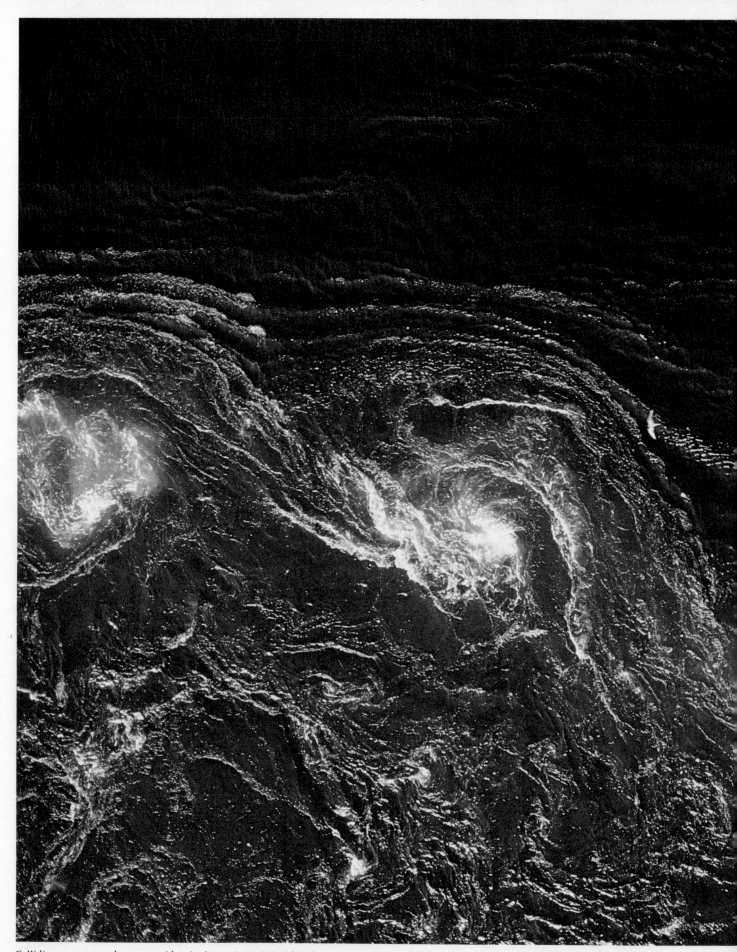

Colliding currents and a strong tide stir the sea into the wild and treacherous eddies of the Maelstrom, the legendary bane of sailors located near the

Lofoten Islands, off the northwest coast of Norway. The thunder of the waters can be heard three miles away.

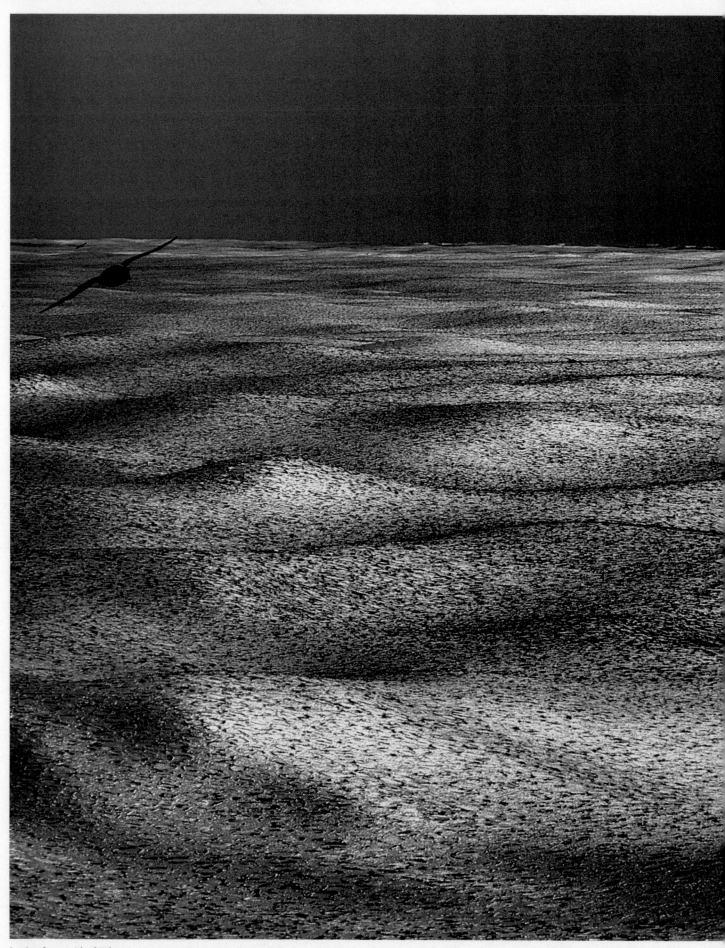

In the deep cold of February, water coalesces into ice crystals on the heaving surface of the Labrador Sea, leaving salts behind in the still-liquid water

below. As its salinity increases, ocean water becomes denser and sinks, setting up a global pattern of deep-sea circulation.

At sunset in the western equatorial Pacific, black thunderclouds developing near the horizon and bands of altocumulus overhead testify to the continuous

exchange of moisture between sea and sky. Water that evaporates and condenses into clouds at cool altitudes eventually returns to the ocean as rain.

Chapter 1

PIONEERS OF A NEW SCIENCE

The scientists who founded the Royal Society of London for Improving Natural Knowledge in 1660 were the intellectual luminaries of the age. Their number included such men as chemist Robert Boyle, Scottish statesman Sir Robert Moray and architect Christopher Wren. And they were also inhabitants of an island nation that had, in the course of several generations, explored the oceans of the world and then extended the power of empire across them. British colonists were flourishing on the North American continent and had pushed south into the West Indies; on the far side of the globe, in the East Indies, Britons were challenging the Dutch for yet another world. It was a time of breathtaking advances in exploration and in scientific knowledge.

But the men of science as yet knew very little about the oceans their country's merchant ships plied. Some studies had been made of coastal shallows and of such small seas as the Mediterranean, but the ships that sailed the great oceans were bent on discovery, conquest and commerce; there was no room on board men-of-war or merchantmen for dabblers in science or their arcane instruments. Given the lack of information, and the importance of the sea to the growth and maintenance of the British Empire, it is small wonder that one of the first orders of business of London's new society was to investigate the oceans that had so far remained beyond the reach of science.

Since they could not go to sea, the fellows of the Royal Society decided to begin their studies by proxy; at their behest, mathematician Lawrence Rooke published in 1662 a list of suggestions as to how mariners could aid scientific inquiry. Rooke requested that they "remark carefully the Ebbings and Flowings of the Sea, in as many places as they can, together with all the Accidents, Ordinary and Extraordinary, of the Tides; To sound and mark the Depths of Coasts and Ports; To take notice of the Nature of the Ground at the bottom of the sea, in all Soundings; To keep a Register of all changes of Wind and Weather at all hours, by night and by day, shewing the point the Wind blows from, whether strong or weak; To carry with them good Scales, and Glasse-Voills of a pint or so, with very narrow mouths, which are to be fill'd with Sea-water, as often as they please, and the weight of the Vial full of water taken exactly at every time, and recorded, marking withall the degree of *Latitude,* and the day of the Month: And that as well of water near the Top; as at a greater Depth." Soon, cooperative sea captains were relaying their observations along with stoppered bottles of ocean water to the scientists back home.

A fearsome whirlpool swallows ships, sailors and houses in this 1935 illustration for Edgar Allan Poe's fanciful short story "Descent into the Maelstrom." The actual whirlpool dramatized by Poe is located off Norway's northwest coast *(pages 8-9)* and is merely turbulence in a strong tidal current, amplified by a rock outcropping that reaches to within 12 feet of the surface.

Although the Royal Society's program was only a beginning, it was an ambitious one and opened lines of investigation that scientists would still be pursuing late in the 20th Century: the nature of sea water, the movements of ocean currents, the configuration of the sea floors and the ways in which the winds and the sea affect each other. It was the first methodical effort to understand the world's oceans.

At the time, the most widely useful advance that had emerged from two centuries of transoceanic voyages was an improvement in mariners' maps. The early Portuguese explorers in the mid-15th Century had been guided by maps that were little changed from those assembled in the Second Century A.D. by the Greco-Egyptian geographer Claudius Ptolemaeus, known as Ptolemy. The ancient charts depicted the lands surrounding the Mediterranean with fair accuracy but greatly overestimated the size of Africa and Asia. The Indian Ocean appeared as a landlocked sea, and the ocean west of Europe as a rather narrow body of water. With a Ptolemaic map in hand, Christopher Columbus calculated that a sea route westward from Europe to the Indies, as Eastern Asia was then called, would be no more than 4,000 miles — 12,000 miles shorter than the arduous overland trade routes that were the only known way to the Indies.

From the time he sailed westward in 1492 to the day of his death, Columbus adhered doggedly to ancient doctrine, maintaining that he had found a new route to Asia and not to a new world. But within a decade of his voyage, Portuguese captains had rounded Africa's Cape of Good Hope and sailed eastward across the Indian Ocean to India and Indonesia. As they traced these new trade routes, Portuguese mapmakers improved on the squat shape Ptolemy had given Africa and gave Asia truer dimensions. The increased knowledge of landforms and distances made it undeniable that Columbus had been wrong; he had in fact discovered a new world.

Some thought it stretched from Pole to Pole and formed an unbreachable barrier between the Atlantic and the Pacific. In 1519 a rugged band of sailors under Captain-General Ferdinand Magellan set out on an audacious attempt to disprove that idea by circumnavigating the globe. Magellan himself did not return from the epic voyage; he was slain by Philippine tribesmen in 1521. But when his crewmen made their way back to Portugal three years later, Europe learned that there was in fact a way past the New World, at the tip of South America. Other voyages of exploration confirmed that the oceans are not discrete bodies of water but merge with one another.

Among the improved 16th Century charts incorporating the hard-won knowledge of the explorers, those of the Flemish cartographer Gerhardus Mercator were the best. Unfortunately, he apparently believed an ancient notion that the earth's surface must be divided equally between land and water, when in fact water covers 72 per cent of the globe. His error prompted him to propose that in the Southern Hemisphere lay a gigantic continent, which he labeled on his maps Terra Australis Incognita — the Unknown Southern Land. Two centuries later his prediction that the continent existed would be proved correct, despite the fact that his assumptions were wrong, his reasoning was flawed, and he had wildly overestimated its size.

Besides limning the outlines of the oceans, Renaissance mariners found a few places at sea where great streams of moving water affected a ship's progress. In many cases, the Europeans were rediscovering what sailors of

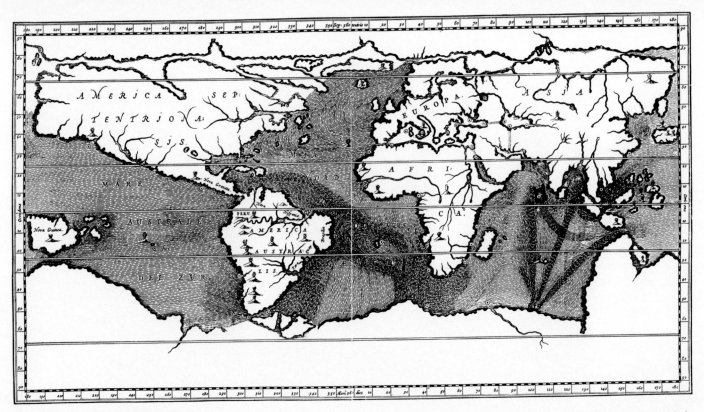

Fact and fancy mingle in this 17th Century map of ocean currents by the German Jesuit Athanasius Kircher. While he was fairly accurate in his depiction of landforms and surface currents, Kircher maintained that the seas were linked by tunnels, including one through the center of the earth from Pole to Pole.

other ages and places had discovered before them. For instance, a 10th Century Indian encyclopedia contains the information that in the Indian Ocean there are currents that change direction with the season. According to veteran Arab sailors consulted by the writer, "the ebb and flow takes place only twice a year in the greatest part of this sea, once in the summer months, then the ebb is six months north-east; and once again in the winter months, then the ebb is six months southwest." It was also well known that the Indian Ocean is swept by monsoons — winds that blow from the northeast in the winter and from the southwest in the summer, paralleling the "ebb and flow" of the currents. (The encyclopedia confused currents with tides, referring to their movements as ebb and flow, as both mariners and scientists would continue to do for centuries.)

European explorers in their turn found currents in the Atlantic. Juan Ponce de León, who searched Florida in vain for the fabled Fountain of Youth, in 1513 discovered off the peninsula's east coast a current so strong that his ships could make no headway, even with a strong wind in their sails. Ponce de León had encountered the southernmost and fastest-flowing segment of the Gulf Stream, a broad current that flows northward from the Caribbean between Florida and Cuba, then turns eastward across the Atlantic. Soon after Ponce de León's discovery, Spanish explorers began using the Gulf Stream to speed their homeward journey.

The men sailing back and forth between the Old and New Worlds recorded in their logs the winds and the water movements they observed, and by 1663 Dutch scholar Isaac Vossius had collected the information contained in generations of captains' and pilots' logs to describe, simply but with reasonable accuracy, a great clockwise flow of intermingled currents in the North Atlantic Ocean. According to Vossius' treatise, "the waters run toward Brazil, along Guyana and enter the Gulf of Mexico. From there, turning obliquely, they pass rapidly through the Straits of Bahama. On the one side they bathe the coasts of Florida and Virginia and the entire shore of North America, and on the other side they run directly east until they reach the opposite shores of Europe and Africa; from thence they run again to the

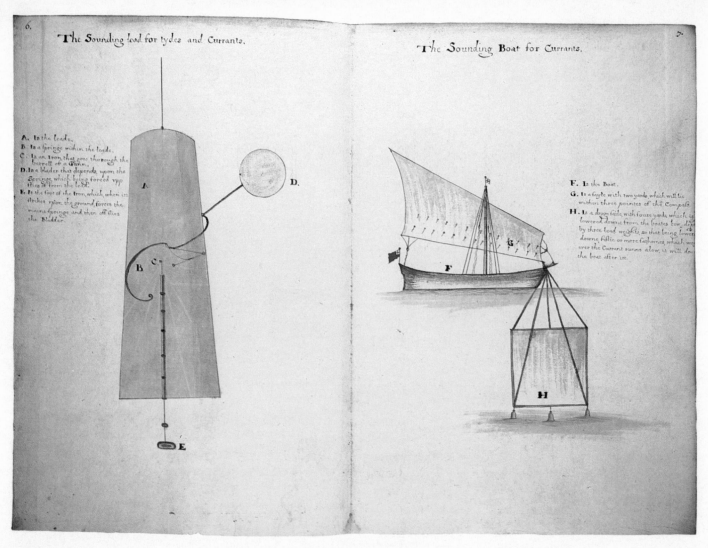

south and join the first movement to the west, perpetually turning in this manner circuitously."

The sudden, marked and often surprising effect on seafarers of these mysterious movements made finding and explaining them a primary objective of the Royal Society. Thus within a year of its inception the society called for an investigation of the strong current that runs from the Atlantic Ocean through the Strait of Gibraltar into the Mediterranean. People had long been puzzled by the fact that so much water flowed continuously into the nearly landlocked sea without raising the sea's level. One explanation offered was that water drained out through some hidden passage in the sea floor, thus preventing the Mediterranean from overflowing. A more plausible idea was that beneath the surface current another flow of water moved in the opposite direction, out into the Atlantic. Several Englishmen living in the British colony of Tangier on the African side of the strait tried to determine whether such an undercurrent existed, but none managed to gather conclusive evidence.

The mystery of the Mediterranean remained unsolved until an inquisitive Italian scientist and soldier successfully analyzed a similar phenomenon at the other end of the Mediterranean. In 1679, twenty-one-year-old Count Luigi Ferdinando Marsili, who had just completed his scientific studies at the University of Padua, offered to accompany an Italian official to Constantinople as an aide. During his stay in the Turkish capital Marsili met the British Ambassador, Sir John Finch, who told the young count that he had been investigating, without conclusion, the waters flowing through the

Illustrated in a 17th Century manuscript, a sounding lead *(above, left)* and an underwater sail *(above)* were designed by British naval officer Richard Bolland to detect hidden currents that might affect navigation. The float on the sounding lead was to be released when the lead touched bottom; current direction would be indicated when the float surfaced.

Bosporus, a channel bordering Constantinople that connects the Black Sea to the Mediterranean. His curiosity piqued, Marsili questioned Turkish fishermen, who confirmed Finch's contention that a surface current and a reverse undercurrent flowed through the Bosporus. When they cast their nets near the surface, the fishermen told Marsili, the nets drifted in the direction of the Mediterranean. But when submerged deeper, the nets were carried in the opposite direction, toward the Black Sea. Not one to go on hearsay, Marsili sank a long line strung with white-painted corks in the Bosporus and observed that in the murky depths the line — made visible by the corks — indeed reversed the direction of its drift.

Marsili suspected that this peculiar phenomenon might be caused by differences in density — or weight per unit volume — between the waters of the Mediterranean and the Black Sea. He knew that the Mediterranean is very salty and reasoned that the Black Sea, since it is fed by many fresh-water streams, would have a lower salt content and thus a lower density. For that reason he assumed that the lighter waters of the Black Sea would flow above the heavier waters of the Mediterranean as the two seas intermingled.

Presumably using the weight of a specific volume of fresh water as a standard, Marsili compared the weights of water samples of equal volume taken at various depths in the Bosporus and from the adjoining seas. He found that the waters of the Black Sea and of the surface current were indeed lighter than were those of the Mediterranean and the eastward-flowing undercurrent.

To test the effects of differing densities on water movement, Marsili designed a model of the Bosporus. He constructed a watertight box with a vertical divider pierced by two holes, one at the top and one at the bottom, which had removable covers. He filled one half of the tank with salt water equal in density to the Bosporus' undercurrent. In the other half, Marsili put colored water that was comparable to the less dense surface current. When he opened the two holes, he could see that the heavy salt water began flowing through the bottom one, forcing the lighter water to move through the top one in the opposite direction. Simply but brilliantly, Marsili had demonstrated for the first time that differences in density can account for movement of water.

Having satisfied his curiosity about the Bosporus, Marsili soon went off to fight the Turks under Holy Roman Emperor Leopold I. Captured and made a slave to a pasha, Marsili managed to escape when the pasha decided that the slaves were a burden and ordered them all decapitated. Marsili was next appropriated by two Bosnian soldiers of fortune, spent a year serving them in miserable conditions and was then ransomed by the same official who had taken him to Constantinople. Marsili returned to his position in Leopold's army, only to be cashiered in 1704 for his role in surrendering a fortress besieged by Spanish troops. His military career behind him, Marsili turned again to scientific pursuits, settling in the French seaside town of Cassis and taking the Mediterranean as his subject.

Marsili's new research program was an ambitious one. "I hope," he wrote, "to treat the nature of the water of the sea and its diverse movements; of the differences of the bottoms of the sea, which seem to me to be related to the structure of the mountains; of the effects of winds on this water; of the nature of fish developments by means of analysis of the vegetation growing on the bottom of the sea." On a number of counts Marsili's research was successful. He was the first scientist to use a dredge to raise marine animals from the bottom and to give a careful description of the flora and fauna of a single region. He recorded the temperature of Mediterranean waters to depths of 300 feet, discovering that while surface readings vary, the temperature below is constant. With sounding lines he detected the shallow sea bottom called the continental shelf that lies between the coastline and the deep sea.

Marsili's studies of the chemistry of sea water and the dynamics of tides and waves were less successful, largely because of the limitations of science in his day. For all his achievements, Marsili recognized that one researcher, working alone, could not hope to make the myriad observations needed to understand the ocean, and he called for government support for oceanic research. That kind of support would not materialize for decades to come. In 1725 Marsili published the results of his solitary studies in his *Physical History of the Sea,* the first volume devoted to the subject. Late in his life, he traveled to London, where he was made a member of the Royal Society and especially welcomed by the great natural philosopher Sir Isaac Newton, who gave a speech lauding Marsili's contributions to science.

One of Marsili's contemporaries had a similar taste for action and science, though he was a less respectable character. William Dampier was an explorer and sometime privateer who ranged both the Atlantic and Pacific, preying on Spanish galleons transporting spices and gold back to Europe. After he returned home to England in 1691, he wrote *A New Voyage round the World,* a picaresque account of his adventures. Its success encouraged him to write a sequel, *Voyages and Discoveries,* which recounted more of his escapades and also included a sober section on his observations of the seas he had sailed. He clearly pointed out the distinction between tides and currents. "By *Tides,*" he wrote, "I mean Flowings and Ebbings of the Sea, on or off any Coast." In contrast: "By *Currents* I mean another Motion of the Sea, which is different from Tides in several Respects, both as to its Duration, and also its Course." A steady transoceanic current, in other words, is quite unlike the local twice-daily periodicity of a tide. Dampier suggested a probable cause of ocean currents: "'Tis generally observed by Seamen, that in all the Places where Trade-winds blow, the Current is influenced by them."

Merchantmen had also come to rely on the steady, predictable trade winds angling toward the Equator in both hemispheres. But they had no idea what generated such winds. In the Fourth Century B.C., Aristotle had proposed that winds were caused by the gravitational effect of the planets revolving around a stationary earth located at the center of the solar system. Almost two millennia later, Columbus believed that this was, in fact, the explanation for the band of steady northeasterly winds he encountered on his voyages between Portugal and America. But in the 16th Century the Polish astronomer Nicholas Copernicus advanced a new concept of the solar system, with the sun at the center, and argued that both the atmosphere and the waters of the oceans move because of the earth's rotation.

But if the earth's rotation were the sole cause of the movement of air and water, winds and currents would move from east to west, parallel to the Equator. Post-Copernican scientists discovered that the sun has a different kind of effect on movements of the atmosphere: They observed that hot air rises and cold, denser air sinks. The flow of cooler air to replace rising warm air is wind. But another problem immediately appeared. If differences in air

Element	Parts per million
Oxygen	857,000
Hydrogen	108,000
Chlorine	19,000
Sodium	10,500
Magnesium	1,350
Sulfur	885
Calcium	400
Potassium	380
Bromine	65
Carbon	28
Strontium	8.1
Boron	4.6
Silicon	3.0
Fluorine	1.3
Argon	.6
Nitrogen	.5
Lithium	.18
Rubidium	.12
Phosphorus	.07
Iodine	.06
Barium	.03
Indium	.02
Zinc	.01
Iron	.01
Aluminum	.01
Molybdenum	.01
Nickel	.0054
Tin	.003
Copper	.003
Arsenic	.003
Uranium	.003
Vanadium	.002
Manganese	.002
Krypton	.0025
Titanium	.001
Cobalt	.00027
Cesium	.0005
Cerium	.0004
Yttrium	.0003
Silver	.0003
Neon	.00014
Cadmium	.00011
Tungsten	.0001
Xenon	.000052
Selenium	.00009
Germanium	.00007
Chromium	.00005
Thorium	.00005
Scandium	.00004
Lead	.00003
Mercury	.00003
Gallium	.00003
Bismuth	.000017
Lanthanum	.000012
Gold	.000011
Thallium	.00001
Helium	.0000069

The table shows all 57 elements that are present in measurable amounts; the quantities given are the number of parts of each element in a million parts of ocean water.

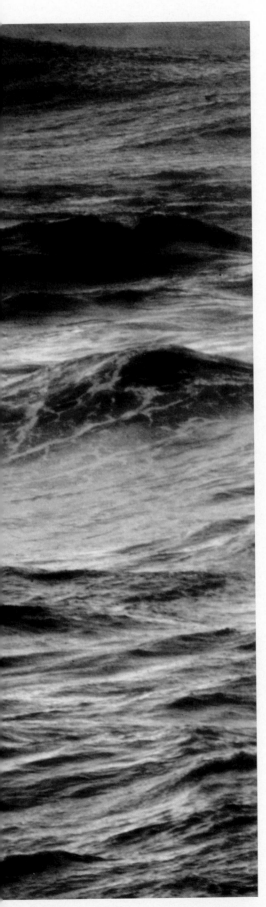

temperature were the primary cause of winds, then in the Northern Hemisphere cold air would flow south from the Pole and warm air north from the Equator. (In the Southern Hemisphere, the directions would be reversed.) Yet, as William Dampier had recorded in his *Voyages and Discoveries,* prevailing winds in the central North Atlantic take a southwestward course, while in the central South Atlantic a northwestward course is the rule.

In 1735 London barrister George Hadley, a fellow of the Royal Society and keeper of its meteorological records, reconciled the two opposing theories of the origins of winds. The surface of the revolving globe, Hadley noted, is moving much more rapidly at the Equator; a point there, on the widest part of the globe, travels through a wider arc in the same time than does a point near the Pole. Thus, when warm air at the Equator rises and flows northward, its eastward momentum makes it take a northeasterly course in relation to the progressively slower-moving earth surface beneath it. Conversely, cold air sinking and flowing southward from the North Pole has less eastward momentum, lags behind the rotating earth and follows a southwesterly course. Thus, near the Equator, the prevailing winds blow from the northeast.

As for the winds, so for the waters. In 1740, the French Royal Academy of Sciences offered four prizes for the best theories explaining ocean tides. Even though Newton had linked the tides to periodic shifts in gravitational forces a half century earlier, there was still confusion among scientists about the distinction between tides and currents. Thus, the academy's contest drew papers on both phenomena. One of the awards was won by another fellow of England's Royal Society, Colin Maclaurin, who built on his colleague Hadley's thesis on winds and showed that the global rotation induced a similar deflection in the oceans' waters. Currents, like winds, are skewed by the rotation of the earth.

As late as the second half of the 18th Century, large expanses of the oceans were still shrouded in mystery — especially the immense reaches of the little-explored South Pacific. No one yet knew whether it harbored the huge undiscovered Terra Australis Incognita or whether such a place was merely a figment of mapmaker Mercator's imagination. In the 17th Century, Dutch explorer Abel Janszoon Tasman had discovered New Zealand, which he took to be a peninsula of the great southern continent. But so many colonies were being established elsewhere, and profitable trade was expanding in so many other directions, that the area was virtually ignored for another century. Then, in 1768, the British Admiralty commissioned Captain James Cook to lead the first of three expeditions to the Pacific. Cook was given several responsibilities. He was to direct astronomical observations for a program designed to establish the diameter of the sun and its distance from the earth. He was also to survey Pacific coastlines and islands and add the features he discovered to existing charts. Not the least of his charges was to search for Terra Australis Incognita and, if he was successful, to claim it for the British Crown.

In all, Cook spent the better part of 10 years crisscrossing the Pacific, making soundings, recording the speeds of currents and winds, and measuring the temperature of ocean waters. He circumnavigated New Zealand, proving it to be a pair of islands and not a peninsula after all. He sailed farther south than anyone before him, crossing the Antarctic Circle and maintaining a poleward course until his progress was barred by ice. Cook saw enough of the icy polar sea — which one of his men described as looking like "the wreck of a shattered world or some region of hell" — to conclude that even if a continent did lie farther south, it was not worth exploring. The Admiralty's hope for a grand new land to enrich the Empire was dashed. Cook resumed his survey of the temperate and tropical reaches of the Pacific and by the time of his death at the hands of Hawaiian islanders in 1779 had charted all of its major elements.

Meanwhile, Benjamin Franklin was adding a major feature to the map of the North Atlantic. The ocean had been heavily traveled for three centuries, and the mariners who, like Ponce de León, had gained direct experience of the great current running along the North American coast, named it the Gulf Stream, presumably because it issues from the Gulf of Mexico. But British chartmakers, oddly enough, ignored the feature when they drew their maps. They were not alone in their ignorance — even Franklin, an avid student of science, was unaware of it until 1768, when he made a trip to London in his capacity as Postmaster General for Britain's American colonies. The Boston Board of Customs had just complained to the Lords of the

The Gulf Stream was mapped for the first time in this 1769 chart by Benjamin Franklin. But for decades afterward ship captains continued to waste weeks sailing against the current on their voyages to America. The "minutes" shown on the chart refer to the current's speed in miles per hour.

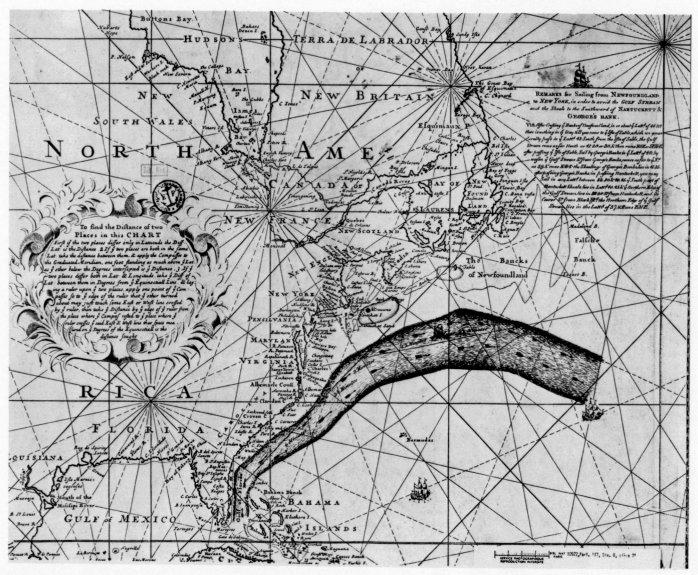

Treasury that British mail packets sailing from England to New York regularly took weeks longer than did the merchant ships to Rhode Island. Their lordships were considering sending packets to Rhode Island instead of New York when one of them asked Franklin about it.

Franklin was puzzled, as he put it, "that there should be such a difference between the two destinations which were scarcely a day's sail apart." Franklin took the problem to a cousin of his, whaling captain Timothy Folger, who happened to be in London at the time. Like all American whalemen, Folger was thoroughly familiar with the Gulf Stream because he had often pursued whales along its boundaries, where the animals fed on plankton. The solution, Folger said, was that the merchant captains, most of them Americans, had learned from the whalemen to avoid the adverse currents of the Gulf Stream on their westward voyage; the British packet captains had not. Even those British who were warned about the stream, Folger added, appeared to ignore it. On more than one occasion, while crossing the stream in pursuit of whales, he and his crew had encountered packets "who were in the middle of it, and stemming it. We have informed them that they were stemming a current, that was against them to the value of three miles an hour; and advised them to cross it and get out of it; but they were too wise to be counselled by simple American fishermen."

To Franklin "it was a pity no notice was taken of this current upon the charts." At Franklin's request, Folger sketched the course of the Gulf Stream on a chart of the Atlantic. Franklin had a local printer make some copies, which he submitted to the Lords of the Treasury with Captain Folger's explanation. The new chart, along with Folger's instructions on how to avoid the stream, was sent to Falmouth for the British packet captains — many of whom paid no attention to it.

As for Franklin, his boundless scientific curiosity had been aroused. On a homeward-bound crossing, he lowered thermometers over the side of his ship and took scores of water-temperature readings, which showed that the Gulf Stream is warmer than the waters bordering it. In 1776, en route to Paris to negotiate a treaty with France, Franklin made more temperature measurements, and in Paris he commissioned another Gulf Stream map, evidently to aid French and American captains carrying arms and supplies to the colonial troops. A decade later, during his return voyage to America, the 79-year-old scientist-diplomat could be seen leaning over the rail of his ship, taking the Gulf Stream's temperature again.

Franklin and Cook had reliable thermometers, as well as the highly accurate clocks called chronometers to measure the speed of currents. Even Marsili, 100 years before, had possessed a reliable hydrometer that helped him determine the density of the waters of the Bosporus. Instruments like these allowed scientists to determine the physical properties of ocean waters. But the study of sea-water chemistry lagged far behind, for lack of adequate tools and techniques. As a result, scientists did not begin to make real progress until the late 18th Century in answering an ancient and basic question about the sea: What makes it salty? In the 1660s, Royal Society fellow Robert Boyle had examined water samples taken from various depths by sea captains during Atlantic crossings. He refuted the notion, commonly held in his day, that beneath a salty surface layer the sea's water was fresh and proved that all sea water is salty. But Boyle's attempts to identify the specific substances that make the water salty failed because of the primitive

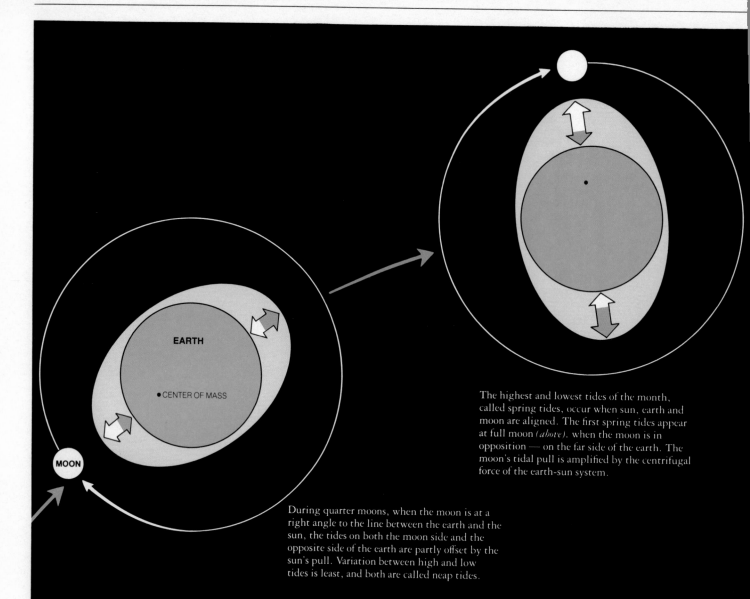

The highest and lowest tides of the month, called spring tides, occur when sun, earth and moon are aligned. The first spring tides appear at full moon *(above).* when the moon is in opposition — on the far side of the earth. The moon's tidal pull is amplified by the centrifugal force of the earth-sun system.

During quarter moons, when the moon is at a right angle to the line between the earth and the sun, the tides on both the moon side and the opposite side of the earth are partly offset by the sun's pull. Variation between high and low tides is least, and both are called neap tides.

The Celestial Mechanics of Tides

Each of the two high tides that occur during the 24 hours 50 minutes it takes the moon to complete an orbit of the earth is a traveling bulge of water. As shown greatly exaggerated in these schematic diagrams (which view the earth's Southern Hemisphere), each bulge is the result of the difference between two forces — the gravitational pull of the moon *(white arrows)* and centrifugal force *(pink arrows).*

Bound together by mutual gravitational attraction, earth and moon spin through space as a single system around a common center of mass located, because of the planet's preponderant size, within the earth. The wobbling of the earth-moon system around this center creates centrifugal force, whose effect on the earth is constant and uniform, and which is directed away from the moon. The moon's gravitational pull exceeds centrifugal force on the nearby earth and pulls the water into the bulge that constitutes one high tide. On the opposite side of the planet, centrifugal force overwhelms gravity, creating the second high tide of the day.

The sun makes a similar contribution to the tidal cycle. But despite its great mass, the sun is so distant that its gravitational and centrifugal effect on earth is slightly less than half that of the moon, and the sun merely augments or diminishes the lunar tides, depending on the alignment of the earth-moon system.

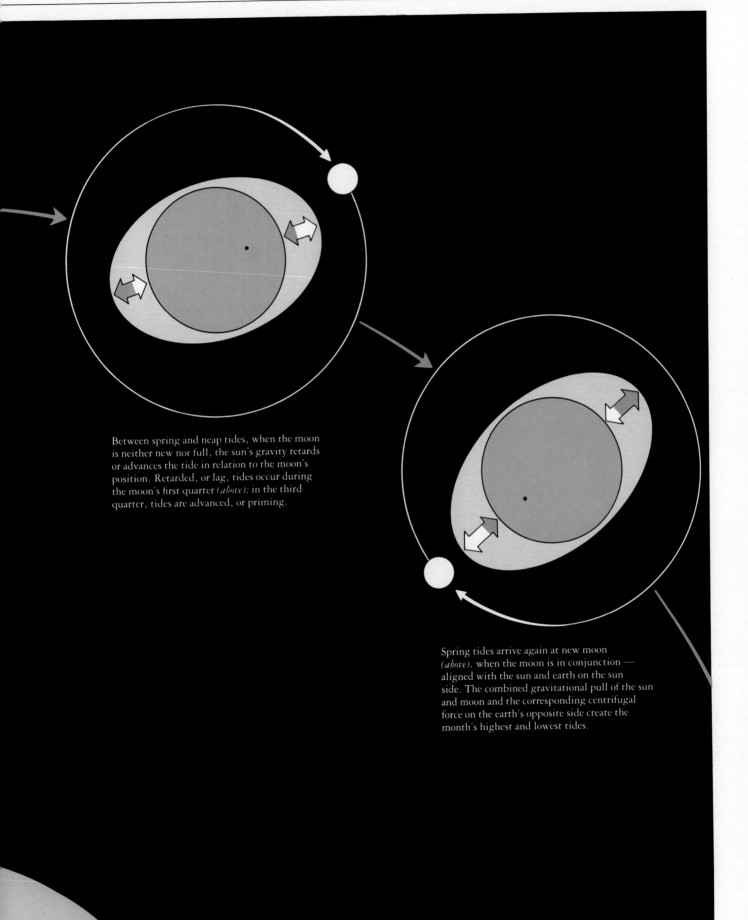

Between spring and neap tides, when the moon is neither new nor full, the sun's gravity retards or advances the tide in relation to the moon's position. Retarded, or lag, tides occur during the moon's first quarter *(above)*; in the third quarter, tides are advanced, or priming.

Spring tides arrive again at new moon *(above)*, when the moon is in conjunction — aligned with the sun and earth on the sun side. The combined gravitational pull of the sun and moon and the corresponding centrifugal force on the earth's opposite side create the month's highest and lowest tides.

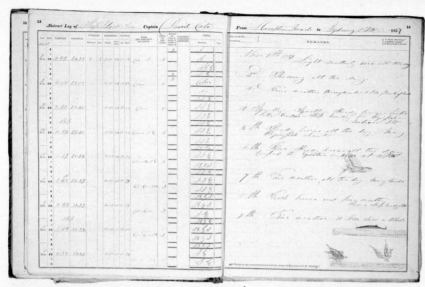

A U.S. Navy cartographer, Lieutenant Matthew Maury (*inset*) won fame in the mid-1800s as the first to attempt a systematic and detailed study of the world's oceanic winds and currents. Maury's technique was simplicity itself and earned him the sobriquet of "armchair oceanographer": He collected thousands upon thousands of ships' logs (*left*), digested their observations and transferred the information onto charts like the one below.

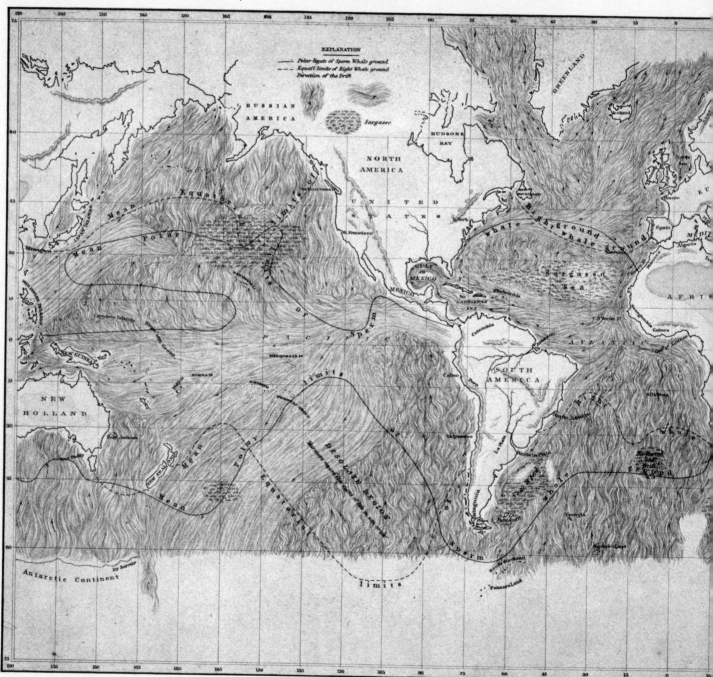

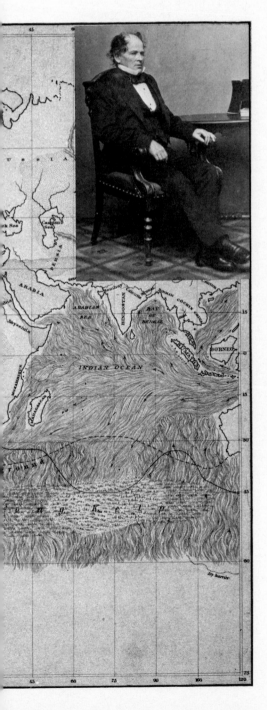

techniques available to him. In the 1770s, however, chemist Antoine Lavoisier reported to the French Royal Academy of Sciences that he had successfully isolated sodium chloride and four other salts from the waters of the English Channel. Tragically, Lavoisier's chemical investigations of sea water were never completed—he was guillotined during the French Revolution because he had been a minor official in the Royalist government.

In post-Revolutionary Europe and America, governments began to follow Britain's lead in sponsoring expeditions like those of Captain Cook. By the early 19th Century, Napoleon had sent two French ships, appropriately named *Le Naturaliste* and *Le Géographe,* on round-the-world explorations. Russian and Danish ships set out with scientists aboard to survey and study the oceans, and the British continued their investigations. The United States was tardy in joining this movement, though President Thomas Jefferson did persuade a reluctant Congress to appropriate federal funds to establish the U.S. Coastal Survey in 1807. Not until 1838 did the first major government-sponsored oceanic expedition set out, under the command of U.S. Navy Lieutenant Charles Wilkes. The staff of the six-vessel expedition included hydrographers (as those who studied the sea were then called), a botanist, a zoologist, a mineralogist and even a philologist to study the languages of the Pacific islanders.

Nearly four years and 80,000 miles later, two of the six ships returned (two had been lost, one sold and one sent home as unseaworthy) with an impressive collection of newly discovered species of flora and fauna, observations of Pacific island cultures and a meticulous compilation of information: 106 new charts of the Pacific and studies of the water depths, temperatures and currents that amounted to the first attempt to assemble a detailed scientific portrait of the Pacific.

But the expedition's return was greeted with apathy and scorn. Wilkes was court-martialed for such offenses as self-aggrandizement (he had promoted himself from lieutenant to captain) and cruelty to his crew (24 lashes instead of the legal 12 to punish his unruly sailors after they helped themselves to the ship's whiskey store and got drunk). Congress had to be persuaded to pay for the publication of the expedition's report. And of the 19 volumes that were finished, 10 were devoted to botany and anthropology, three to ethnological studies and the rest to miscellaneous subjects. Only one, by Wilkes, covered the study of the ocean itself. Because of his other troubles, it took him 30 years to finish this volume, by which time most of the findings were out of date.

In the decade following Wilkes's expedition, other Americans headed surveys of the East and West coasts of the United States; a study of the Japan Current, the Pacific Ocean's counterpart to the Gulf Stream; and even, oddly enough, of the Dead Sea. But the era's most productive American hydrographer accomplished his contribution to charting the waters of the world without leaving his desk in Washington.

Matthew Fontaine Maury had commenced his studies of the oceans' winds and currents as a young navigator in the U.S. Navy. In 1839, however, en route from his family home in Tennessee to New York for sea duty, he was thrown from a toppling stagecoach and broke his right thigh. The injury left Maury with a bad limp, and the Navy concluded that he could not serve aboard ship. Three years after his accident, Maury was made superintendent

H.M.S. *Challenger* (*left*) plows through heavy seas in a painting done to commemorate her 41-month oceanographic expedition, which began in 1872. During the voyage a research team led by Charles Wyville Thomson (*below, second from right*) made voluminous observations and dredged up thousands of previously unknown sea creatures.

of the U.S. Navy's Depot of Charts and Instruments, which was the repository for all the logbooks that had been kept by Navy vessels since the service's formation. Another duty of the depot was to issue charts of the ocean for the Navy, and Maury soon discovered that little information was available for this activity. In fact, as he pointed out to his superiors, most of the charts used by the U.S. Navy had been compiled by European chart makers. He soon realized that a solution to this problem was at hand—in the neglected piles of logbooks.

With the Navy's blessing, he set his assistants to work sorting through this mountain of data. Many of the logbook entries were cryptic, but by carefully winnowing out all of the wind and current observations, and then organizing them geographically, Maury began to compile a useful body of information. He also conceived the idea of issuing special "abstract logs" to Navy and merchant captains, requesting them to use the 12 blank pages at the end of each log to record information on certain currents, winds, water temperatures and other relevant phenomena. Some of the captains were slow to grasp the point of this new duty and failed to fill out the abstract logs. But Maury and his workers had plenty of material in the stored logbooks for the first edition of *Wind and Current Charts,* which was published in 1847. When one merchant skipper, employing the new charts, cut 35 days off the usual 110-day round-trip run between Baltimore and Rio de Janeiro, the demand for Maury's charts soared; and when Maury responded by offering free copies of his publications to captains who filled out his abstracts, the data began to pour in.

But Maury wanted still more detail on current movements, and he came up with a novel method for obtaining it. He persuaded sailors to make occasional notations of their ship's position. This information was to be dated and put on a piece of paper containing a request that anyone who found the note return it to Maury in Washington along with word on where it had been found; the sailor then sealed the paper in a bottle and tossed it overboard, to be swept away by currents. Soon many of these bottles were picked up and their contents returned, enabling Maury to add more information on the general direction and speed of currents in his charts.

Maury was soon able to describe the changes in circulation of the major ocean currents by season. By 1851, such information was helping American clipper ship captains cut a month or more off their three-month races to the gold fields of California, and scores of grateful skippers were sending their observations to Maury's depot. Two years later, Maury was able to prove the value of his findings by meeting a dramatic challenge.

In January of 1854, the brig *Napoleon* raced into New York Harbor with a report that she had sighted the ship *San Francisco,* dismasted by a storm and drifting in mid-Atlantic. The seas had been too high for the *Napoleon* to effect a rescue. While the Navy readied two swift cutters to rush to the *San Francisco's* aid, Maury studied his charts, estimated the direction of the Gulf Stream currents, calculated the drift of the dismasted hulk and drew an X where he thought the ship would be by the time the rescuers arrived. The cutters found the still-drifting *San Francisco* at almost exactly the spot Maury had indicated.

By now known as the "Pathfinder of the Seas" in every maritime nation, Maury also conceived the idea of the first international conference on ocean science. The International Maritime Meteorological Conference was attended by representatives from 10 countries when it convened in Brussels in August of 1853. The delegates unanimously agreed on a standardized system of collecting scientific observations, largely in the form of Maury's abstract logs. By the next year, 90 per cent of the world's navigators were sending their reports to Washington—and finding the effort well worthwhile. British shippers alone estimated that with the help of Maury's *Wind and Current Charts* they were saving $10 million a year.

Besides organizing information into a form that made sea voyages faster and safer, Maury pored over deep soundings made from Navy ships to draw a contour map of a section of the Atlantic Ocean basin, on a line running from Yucatan to the Cape Verde Islands off the west coast of Africa. Though sketchy by modern standards, Maury's map indicated an elevated area in midocean that he named the Dolphin Rise, after the ship from which the soundings were made. This was the first hint of the existence of the tremendous feature later found to rise a mile above the ocean floor and stretch the length of the Atlantic Ocean—the mid-Atlantic Ridge.

Maury did not rest content with his great work as a compiler of information. In 1855, he published *The Physical Geography of the Sea,* which presented solid information on currents, winds, ocean depths and weather—along with his explanations for these phenomena. Brilliant as Maury was, however, his grounding in physics and other disciplines was not good enough to enable him to construct useful theories, and scientists with more academic training scorned his conclusions. Not long afterward, he sided with his native South at the commencement of the Civil War. He was denounced as a traitor, and publication of his *Wind and Current Charts* was suspended until 1883, ten years after his death.

During the years when Maury was charting the surface movements of the oceans, a brilliant naturalist from the University of Edinburgh was advancing some intriguing theories about the depths of the sea. In 1841, on a voyage aboard Britain's Navy surveying ship *Beacon* in the eastern Mediterranean, 26-year-old Edward Forbes was trying to secure samples of marine life from the sea bottom, 780 feet down. But his nets and dredges brought up virtually no fish. Similar dredges in the shallower waters off Britain had

In 1871, with the "cordial assent of the House of Commons" to provide funds, Charles Wyville Thomson of the Royal Society of London began preparations for an epic voyage of scientific investigation. He crammed a 226-foot Navy vessel, H.M.S. *Challenger,* with laboratories, workrooms, cabins and special decks. Then, as the Admiralty put it, she was fitted with "all the instruments and apparatus which modern science and practice have been able to suggest and devise." The equipment ranged from a compact laboratory for analyzing sea water to enormous reels of thick rope — at least eight miles of it — for retrieving samples from the deep ocean floor.

The difficulties were prodigious. The ship itself was slow and clumsy, with a tendency to roll alarmingly; most of the instruments, although state of the art, were inaccurate and frequently failed altogether. Yet during their three-and-a-half-year, 68,890-mile voyage the *Challenger's* plucky crew discovered myriad new forms of life in the deep, obtained extensive profiles of deep-water temperatures and movements and charted accurately the principal surface currents of the world. "Never did an expedition cost so little," said a member of the Royal Society later, "and produce such momentous results for human knowledge."

The *Challenger's* tiny chemistry laboratory boasts four work surfaces, a glass-blowing shop, a sink, numerous burners and space for storing hundreds of chemicals. Made to illustrate the expedition's official report, this engraving and the one below were based on sketches drawn during the voyage.

In the more spacious naturalists' workroom on board the *Challenger,* two members of the scientific team use microscopes to examine minute fossils dredged from the ocean floor.

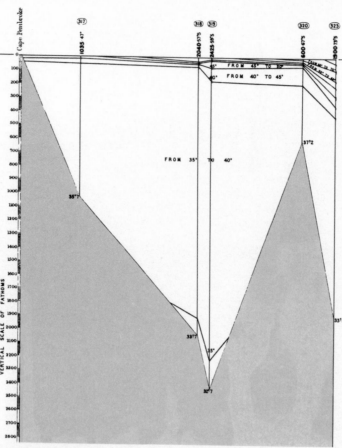

A sea thermometer *(left)*, protected from water pressure by a copper case, records maximum and minimum temperatures with floats that remain at the extremities reached by the mercury. A chart of the instrument's readings *(above)* shows water temperatures at various depths between the Falkland Islands *(left margin)* and Montevideo *(right)*.

Chemist John Buchanan *(right)* measures the density of sea water in a hydrometer. To collect samples, a crewman lowered a stopcock bottle *(above, right)* to the desired depth with valves open at both ends. As soon as he began pulling the bottle up, water resistance forced the controlling arm down, closing the valves.

A crewman empties the contents of a townet into a jar as members of the scientific team examine other specimens. The *Challenger's* biological researchers identified thousands of species and proved that life forms inhabit even the deepest reaches of the sea.

A five-stage diagram *(below)* shows how the *Challenger's* deep-sea dredge was lowered to the ocean floor. A heavy weight *(labeled G)* partway down the towrope dragged both the rope and the dredge to the bottom. There the weight converted the ship's diagonal pulling force to the horizontal, keeping the dredge at the proper attitude for scooping up material.

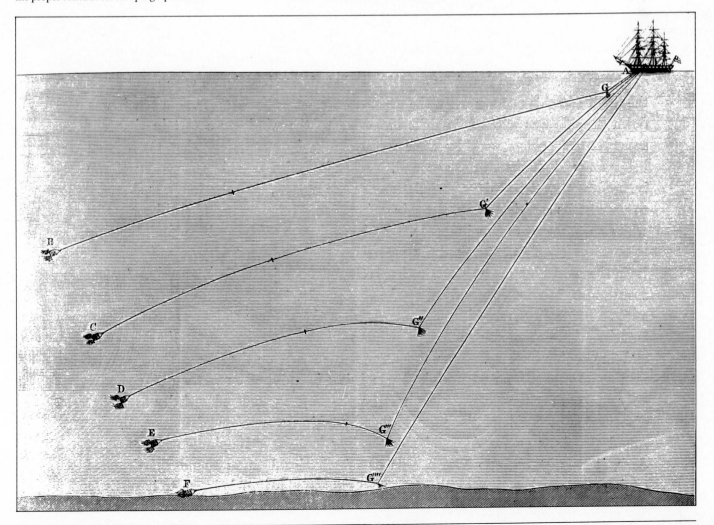

been far more productive. On the basis of these and other observations, Forbes concluded that the quantity of flora and fauna in the ocean diminishes with increasing depth. He reasoned that the plants disappear first as the water becomes darker, because they must have sunlight for photosynthesis. Next the small animals dependent on plants begin to vanish; then the fish that feed on the small animals disappear. Forbes maintained that the chance of any life existing at depths of more than 1,800 feet — a region that he called the azoic zone — was a "probable zero."

Forbes died in 1854 at the age of 39. But his zone theory, and especially his claim that no life existed in the abyss, endured until another brilliant scholar from Edinburgh, Charles Wyville Thomson, set out to test it further. In 1868, Thomson went out in the *Lightning,* the most ancient paddle steamer in the British Navy, to dredge the bottom of the North Atlantic off Scotland. He brought up many different samples of shrimp, sea urchins and other creatures from depths down to 650 fathoms, or 3,900 feet. "A grand new field of inquiry has been opened up," Thomson wrote. At his urging, the Admiralty agreed to sponsor an ambitious around-the-world deep-sea expedition that would last several years. In 1872 the 42-year-old Thomson took command of the research vessel *Challenger* and sailed from Portsmouth, England.

Just as the American Wilkes expedition had embraced many fields of study, so the *Challenger's* mission went beyond dredging the deep — coming to include surveys of surface movements of the oceans as well as studies of life and physical conditions in the depths. The ship was fitted out below-decks with a zoological laboratory for examining specimens brought up from the sea, as well as a library, workrooms and staterooms for the six scientists aboard.

Up-to-date instruments of all sorts were aboard the *Challenger.* One was a thermometer that enabled researchers to take accurate temperature readings on or near the ocean bottom; previous attempts to retrieve such data had frequently been stymied when the water pressure at great depths distorted the reading or crushed the instrument altogether. The *Challenger's* deep-sea thermometers were sheathed in copper tubes that protected the delicate instruments from destructive pressure so that they could register precise temperatures.

Using these rugged gauges, scientists of the *Challenger* expedition made a significant finding. A worldwide series of temperature readings showed that deep water is cold in all of the oceans, regardless of season or surface temperature. The scientists also noted that this water is coldest near the Antarctic and that temperatures gradually increase in a northerly direction. This was an early indication that frigid Antarctic water flows slowly toward the Equator from the southern oceans.

Besides measuring the physical properties of the sea, the scientists of the *Challenger* investigated its chemistry. Much was already known about the make-up of the oceans; by the 1860s, chemists had isolated 27 elements in sea water, and the Danish mineralogist Georg Forchhammer had concluded that the ratio of sea salts to one another remains virtually constant across the oceans' entire surface. But the *Challenger's* researchers were able to expand on the Dane's work. In addition to taking surface samples — all that Forchhammer had had to work with — they took samples from depths down to 1,000 fathoms and more and turned them over to chemist William Dittmar for analysis. In his report, which was not published until 1884, Dittmar confirmed Forchhammer's conclusion about surface ratios, and extended it to all depths of the ocean.

The *Challenger* also took along a sounding device to be lowered on thin, lightweight piano wire instead of the cumbersome hemp rope used to take soundings since Ferdinand Magellan's attempt to locate the bottom of the Pacific three and a half centuries earlier. Unfortunately, the wire tangled so badly that the reel on which it was wound collapsed, and the men had to rely solely on conventional rope, lowered and cranked up with a steam-operated winch. Despite this setback, the *Challenger's* researchers were able to plumb impressive depths. In 1875, off the Marianas Islands in the Pacific, they made their deepest sounding, hitting bottom at an amazing 26,850 feet — more than five miles.

Marine biology also took a great leap forward with the *Challenger* voyage. In all, the ship's scientists collected 4,417 new species of plants and animals — "strange and beautiful things," Thomson wrote, "which seemed to give us a glimpse of the edge of some unfamiliar world." One hundred thirty-three dredge hauls, some of them reaching to depths of 2,000 feet, proved beyond a doubt that Forbes's theory of the azoic zone was mistaken. (Forbes had been misled by the fact that he had by chance done his dredging in a barren part of the Mediterranean.) The zoologists aboard also disposed of another erroneous idea. In the 1860s, engineers laying a telegraph cable off the Canadian coast had preserved in alcohol a sample of material dredged up from the ocean floor. Taken back to England, the slimy, amorphous stuff was examined by the great naturalist Thomas Henry Huxley, who concluded that it was the most primitive form of life ever discovered. He named the substance bathybius, which means in Greek "life of the deep," and speculated that a thin layer of it covers the entire ocean floor. In all their dredgings, the *Challenger* scientists found no bathybius in the sea — but they did find it in their specimen bottles. They discovered that when alcohol is used to preserve sea-bottom specimens in sea water, calcium and sulfur compounds precipitate and sink to the bottom in a shapeless mass of slime. The engineers had presented Huxley not with a new life form but with a chemical accident.

The scientists and crewmen of the *Challenger* were welcomed home enthusiastically from their 68,890-mile voyage on May 24, 1876, and with good reason. Thomson and his staff had compiled enough notes, journals and logbooks for an unprecedented 50-volume dossier on the oceans. Thomson, who was knighted for his service to science, set about sifting through the mass of information, but he died in 1882 before the great task was completed. The final volume of the *Challenger Report* was not published until 1895, almost 20 years after the ship's return.

Long before then, however, scientists recognized the revolutionary importance of Thomson's accomplishment. Indeed, just two months after the *Challenger* returned home, Thomas Huxley remarked at a dinner honoring the ship's staff that before the expedition "a foundation for future thought upon the physical geography of the sea not only had not existed, but had not even been dreamed of." Ω

Chapter 2

SECRETS OF THE OCEAN CURRENTS

In the 1890s, no one knew whether or not there was a major ocean beneath the eternal shroud of ice that encased the top of the world. Some scientists believed that there must be land under the polar icecap; others assumed that if there were an Arctic Ocean, it could be no more than a shallow sea strewn with shoals and islands.

The Norwegian explorer and zoologist Fridtjof Nansen, who in 1888 had made the first crossing of the Greenland icecap, brought his Arctic experience to the debate. Aware that driftwood from Siberia collected on the eastern shores of Greenland, more than 5,000 miles to the west, he concluded — and proclaimed confidently — that there was indeed a great ocean in the Arctic, and that its uncharted currents carried both the driftwood and the great masses of ice that all but covered the sea. To prove his assertion, the venturesome Nansen proposed to make a remarkable odyssey — he would sail into the ice, let his ship become trapped in it, and see where the ice took him. Eventually, the expedition would settle far more than just the question of an Arctic current, for Nansen's careful observations of ice movement would lead to a breakthrough in understanding the ceaseless flow of surface circulation in every ocean in the world.

Backed with capital from the Norwegian Parliament and private subscription, and imbued with confidence, Nansen made arrangements for his voyage. He designed a ship that would be "able to slip like an eel out of the embrace of the ice," as he described it. Christened *Fram,* Norwegian for "forward," the 128-foot schooner boasted a blunt-ended hull made of oak planks four feet thick, encased in greenheart — a wood so dense that it does not float — and reinforced with massive beams crisscrossing the 36-foot-wide interior.

The *Fram* nosed out of harbor in Vardo, Norway, on July 27, 1893, sailed east along the Siberian coast toward the New Siberian Islands, then set a northward course. Nansen took along 34 sled dogs; if the *Fram* drifted near enough, he intended to try to reach the North Pole over ice.

The ship sailed northward unimpeded for nearly three months before encountering the first signs of ice — which then closed in with terrifying force. As Nansen wrote in his journal, "The ice is pressing and packing around us with a noise like thunder. It is piling itself up into long walls, and heaps high enough to reach a good way up the *Fram's* rigging; in fact, it is trying its very utmost to grind the *Fram* into powder." But the stout hull withstood the test. By mid-October the *Fram* was locked in Arctic ice and was indeed drifting with the currents, as Nansen had prophesied.

A stripe of coral larvae marks the convergence of two surface currents in the Atlantic near Bermuda. The normally well-dispersed larvae are concentrated into a visible band where the currents collide and sink.

Eager to learn where the ice was taking them, the crew gathered daily as sightings were taken to fix their position. For several days, they moved slowly southward, then to the east, after which the ice and its prisoner shifted course again and headed north.

Except for the ceaseless cacophony of howling blizzard and grinding ice, the 13-member crew of the *Fram* found life in their ice-locked world uneventful. They took periodic measurements of the ocean's temperature, salinity and currents at different depths through holes drilled in the ice and occasionally tramped across the ice pack to hunt polar bear.

The ship moved much more slowly than Nansen had expected and in January 1894, he learned the probable reason: The ocean bottom dropped away to a depth far greater than he had anticipated, beyond the reach of the ship's sounding line. Nansen now estimated the bottom to be 2,000 fathoms, or more than two miles, down. "In one point only have my calculations proved incorrect," he wrote, "but unfortunately in one of the most important. I presupposed a shallow Polar Sea. I reasoned that all currents would have a strong influence." Instead, the Arctic currents, diffused in a deep sea, were moving almost imperceptibly. Through the rest of 1894, the *Fram* sat nearly motionless.

In early 1895 the schooner began moving faster, and by March Nansen calculated that the *Fram* was about 360 miles from the North Pole. Selecting crew member Frederik Johansen to accompany him, Nansen decided to set out for the Pole on foot. He instructed the captain of the *Fram* to attempt to break free of the ice and head for home as soon as

Locked in Arctic ice, the Norwegian schooner *Fram* is actually moving at the rate of about one mile per day during an 1893-1896 expedition that proved the existence of a powerful circumpolar ocean current. The windmill visible on the deck provided electricity.

Norwegian scientist Fridtjof Nansen is shown here in 1888 after becoming the first person to cross the forbidding Greenland icecap. Nansen postulated the existence of the circumpolar current and led the *Fram* on its remarkable voyage of discovery.

summer arrived. And on March 14, Nansen and Johansen embarked on their journey, equipped with two sleds, the sled dogs, a kayak and a small amount of provisions.

A month of trekking across the ice took the explorers to within 225 miles of the Pole, closer than anyone had been before, but the journey was an arduous one; they had planned to supplement their food supply by hunting, but game proved almost nonexistent and the men had to eat their dogs to survive. Ultimately, the jagged ridges of ice presented too great an obstacle and they abandoned their quest. Heading south in search of land and game, the men fought their way 400 miles to an island where, in August, they built a hut and sat out the winter.

In the spring of 1896, the ice started to break up, and Nansen and Johansen set out again in their light boat. They had been pushing their way through ice floes for weeks when one morning Nansen heard a dog bark and pulled ashore on an island. He and Johansen shouted and were answered by a man's voice.

The explorers, ragged and dirty, staggered up the beach to be greeted by a clean-shaven, scented Englishman wearing a checked suit. Without hesitation, the stranger asked, "Aren't you Nansen? I'm Jackson of the Jackson-Harmsworth Polar Expedition. By Jove, I'm glad to see you."

Frederick Jackson explained that they had reached Franz Josef Land and that his expedition was attempting to see if the archipelago stretched all the way to the North Pole. Nansen was able to tell him authoritatively that it did not. Nansen and Johansen returned home in August 1896 on Jackson's supply ship. A few days after their arrival in Norway, they were greeted with a telegram from Spitsbergen: *FRAM* ARRIVED IN GOOD CONDITION. ALL WELL ON BOARD.

During the nearly two years that Nansen and Johansen had been away from her, the *Fram* had drifted 1,028 miles, mostly southwest, at an average speed of about one mile per day. During the first summer, the schooner was unable to get far enough south before another winter set in. Not until the summer of 1896 did the *Fram* finally reach ice-free water and sail for home.

In summing up his extraordinary adventure afterward, Nansen wrote, "What, then, are the results of the Norwegian Polar Expedition? In the first place, we have demonstrated that the sea in the immediate neighborhood of the Pole, and in which, in my opinion, the Pole itself in all probability lies, is a deep basin, not a shallow one." The meandering *Fram,* which had made its icebound way from Asia to Europe, had convinced Nansen that "drift ice is continually moving from one side of the Polar basin north of the Bering Strait and the coast of Siberia, across the regions around the Pole, and out toward the Atlantic Ocean."

More important, Nansen pointed out, was the proof that the ice did move. Nansen and his stout little schooner had, as he proudly put it, "gone far to lift the veil of mystery which has hitherto shrouded these regions." The Arctic Ocean was not a shallow, frozen barrier to the circulation of the oceans but a moving, integral part of a circulatory system that was, it could now be argued convincingly, truly global in scale. Sixty-five years later, nuclear submarines would prove Nansen's contention that a major current flows northward over the Pole, but the submarines did it by traveling beneath the ice from one side of the globe to the other. While the immedi-

ate accomplishments of Nansen's expedition were considerable, the most remarkable scientific contribution of the voyage would not be realized for several years.

At the time of Nansen's voyage, scientists had fairly sophisticated theories about ocean circulation but a far from complete picture of its intricate mechanics. One of the basic principles of those mechanics had been established in 1856 by an American physicist, William Ferrel. While an extreme shyness kept Ferrel, a West Virginia schoolteacher, from ever seeking the scientific limelight, his mathematical brilliance nevertheless catapulted him to world prominence in geophysical fluid dynamics. Ferrel was the first to apply to the movement of the seas a mathematical theory that had been advanced 20 years before by France's Gaspard de Coriolis.

Coriolis' calculations had shown that the path of a body in motion on a spinning surface curves in relation to any other body on the same surface. The point can be illustrated by considering a hypothetical baseball hurled toward the North Pole by someone standing at the Equator. As it began its northward flight, the baseball would also be traveling eastward with the spinning globe at approximately 1,050 miles per hour. Toward the Pole, because the earth's circumference is smaller, the surface is moving at a slower rate; at lat. 30° N., for example, its velocity is approximately 935 miles per hour. But as the baseball moved northward, unattached to the earth and therefore unaffected by the diminishing circumference, it would still be flying eastward at 1,050 miles per hour. Viewed from space above

A Finnish research vessel moves with drifting ice in the Baltic Sea during a study of ice formation in the 1970s. A wind mast planted on the ice measures wind velocity at different levels for correlation with ice movements.

the earth, the baseball would appear to be moving north in a straight line, but to an observer on earth the ball would appear to curve to the right. (A baseball hurled toward the South Pole would appear to curve to the left.) The deflection increases as the ball travels farther from the Equator. The effect is to curve the ball clockwise in the Northern Hemisphere and in a counterclockwise direction south of the Equator. By applying the Coriolis effect to winds and ocean currents, Ferrel was able to explain the clockwise movement of currents in the Northern Hemisphere and their counterclockwise flow in the Southern Hemisphere.

After a study of some observations made early in the century, Ferrel also theorized that one effect of the earth's rotation on the warm water at the Equator would be to cause the water to accumulate in midocean, at about lat. 28°. Since warm water expands and is lighter than cold, Ferrel surmised that this accumulation would form a hill of water rising about five feet above the level of the sea at the Equator. This build-up, he contended, would be balanced by a flow of deep water away from the accumulation—a result of the weight of the hill of water.

Much was learned during Ferrel's time about the location and direction of the world's ocean currents; but explaining why they flowed as they did proved much more difficult. Theorists soon divided into two camps: One group held that strong prevailing winds, such as the trade winds, drove surface waters; and the other believed that differences in temperature and density set the sea in motion.

In 1870, the respected English biologist William B. Carpenter, whose deep-ocean collecting expeditions with Charles Wyville Thomson aboard the *Porcupine* had proved that life exists in the depths, joined the debate. He asserted that currents began as a vertical circulation between the Equator and the Poles; the sinking of cold, dense polar waters, he said, drew toward the Poles the warm, less dense water from the Equator.

The scholarly Carpenter was immediately challenged by an unlikely opponent—an unschooled Scottish geologist, James Croll. Not one to feel inhibited by his lack of formal education, the well-read and logically adept Croll engaged some of the foremost thinkers of his day in spirited debate. Croll was a proponent of the popular wind-stress theory of current flow, which held that, in the case of the Atlantic, prevailing westerlies built up in the Gulf of Mexico a hill of water that would run downhill at a speed proportionate to the height to which it had been driven, flowing out of the Gulf and northeastward along the North American coast as the water sought to level itself. In correspondence and publications, Croll and Carpenter exchanged fusillades for several years, but neither had the tools to prove his point.

While the debate about the causes of the currents awaited resolution, a princely scientist bankrolled by the gaming tables of Monte Carlo devised a novel experiment to learn more about the course of currents in the Atlantic Ocean. Prince Albert of Monaco had an enormous income at his disposal. By the age of 25 he had tired of repeated pleasure cruises on his yacht *Hirondelle,* but he had become curious about the sea itself. Thus, when Professor Georges Pouchet of the Paris Museum of Natural History proposed an investigation into the currents of the eastern Atlantic, Albert was eager to participate.

At the time, oceanographers were engaged in a lively controversy over the terminus of the Gulf Stream. A number of scientists argued that the stream dissipated by the time it reached the eastern Atlantic; others maintained that it divided, some of its water swinging north around the British Isles and the rest traveling south along the European coast. Hoping to settle the controversy, Prince Albert took the *Hirondelle* out through the Strait of Gibraltar in the summer of 1885. Aboard were Professor Pouchet and an array of curious devices: 150 glass bottles, 10 hollow, watertight copper spheres and 20 beer barrels. In each of these floats was a request, printed in 10 languages, that the finder send details of its discovery to Prince Albert at Monte Carlo. Heading westward, the *Hirondelle* sailed to the Azores, where Albert tossed 169 of the bottles and barrels over the vessel's side and watched them bob away.

The following year he took more than 500 bottles out into the Atlantic, turned northward and released them along a route between Spain and the English Channel. The next year, more than 900 bottles went over the *Hirondelle's* sides as the yacht cruised from the Azores westward to the Grand Banks off North America.

In all, Prince Albert released 1,675 bottles and barrels; 1,448 were lost but reports on the other 227 bottles made the Prince's experiment worth the effort and expense. Charting the travels of each float indicated the existence of two major currents in the eastern Atlantic, one curving northeastward past Great Britain and one turning southeastward along the European coast. Moreover, since two of the floats released off France were picked up across the Atlantic in the West Indies, Prince Albert concluded that the southern arm joins the westward-flowing North Equatorial Current to form an enormous gyre encircling the North Atlantic. After World War I, Albert would use insights gained from his experiment to warn shippers of drifting mines; at least 60 mines were eventually found on beaches on both sides of the Atlantic, having followed the drift patterns Prince Albert projected.

By the end of the 19th Century, scientists had established that currents moved in oceanwide gyres and theorized that water density played a role in powering those currents. Then, a particular observation made by Fridtjof Nansen aboard the *Fram* and published six years after the expedition triggered the next major advance in understanding how the whole system works. Nansen reported that the icebound *Fram* had not drifted with the winds but had followed a course that was between 20 and 40 degrees to the right of the wind direction. Nansen described this deflection—which he attributed to the Coriolis effect—to physicist Vagn Walfrid Ekman, and speculated that deeper layers of ocean must be deflected in the same way. Nansen thought that as each layer of water was dragged into motion by friction with the moving layer above it, the Coriolis effect would deflect it to the right. Because of the energy lost to friction, the deeper the layer of water the slower its movement would be. Eventually, he proposed, a layer about 300 feet deep would flow almost imperceptibly in nearly the opposite direction of the wind that had set the surface water in motion.

Ekman translated Nansen's thoughts into a mathematical model that confirmed the basic idea and showed that the average movement of an entire column of wind-driven water is at right angles to the direction of the wind, 90 degrees to the right in the Northern Hemisphere and 90 degrees to the

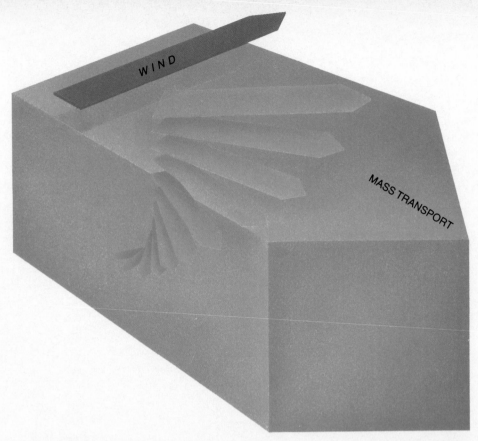

As wind drives surface currents, the underlying water is set in motion by friction and deflected by the Coriolis effect. With increasing depth each layer is deflected more and moves more slowly, until about 350 feet down a weak current moves upwind. The overall result of this so-called Ekman spiral is to move water at right angles to the wind.

left in the Southern Hemisphere. Ekman's theory describes successive layers of moving water twisted like a spiral staircase, a model that has come to be known as the Ekman spiral. So many other factors influence the movement of ocean water that a classic Ekman spiral would never be observed in the sea. But as a theoretical model, it helped to explain several mystifying characteristics of moving water.

Most significantly, the spiral showed how Ekman transport — the average movement of water at right angles to the prevailing winds — builds up a mound of water as much as six feet high near the center of each ocean basin, the phenomenon predicted by William Ferrel more than 50 years earlier. The importance of the hills was finally realized in 1909 when two Scandinavian oceanographers finally resolved the debate over the driving force of currents — in a way that supported elements of the arguments advanced by both Croll and Carpenter. Johan Sandstrom and Björn Helland-Hansen concluded that the vast current gyres in the oceans actually revolve with the midocean mounds of water as their hubs. As Sandstrom and Helland-Hansen reasoned, adjacent water masses having different densities, determined by their temperature and salinity, tend to move relative to one another in response to horizontal pressure — the tendency of water to seek its own level. That movement must be influenced by the Coriolis effect, but in a far more complicated interchange than Croll and Carpenter ever imagined.

As Croll and other proponents of wind stress noted, the major currents of the world follow the large-scale atmospheric patterns of prevailing winds. Those winds move water that, because it is heated by the sun, is less dense than the water below it. As explained by the Ekman spiral, this upper-ocean water, deflected to the right of the winds, tends to move northward from the trade winds and southward from the westerlies — hence a build-up of water in the calmer latitudes between the wind belts.

Gravity impels water to level out, drawing it downhill, as Carpenter had insisted; the omnipresent Coriolis effect deflects this movement to the

Fresh water from New Zealand's Clarence River, lighter in color and less dense than sea water, overrides the darker brine of the Pacific Ocean. Depending

on the strength of the currents along the coast, river discharge may take months or even years to mix into the open ocean.

right. The contesting forces produce a circular flow — the geostrophic current — along the subtle contours of the mound of water. Specifically, what Sandstrom and Helland-Hansen developed was an equation for altering current speed and direction based on the elevation of the central mound, which can be calculated from the density of the water. (Nearly 70 years later, the hills of water, a theoretical presumption for more than a century, were directly observed for the first time. The Seasat satellite, utilizing precision altimetry, revealed a gentle slope of 4.7 feet rising from the outer to the inner edge of the Gulf Stream.)

The geostrophic equation enabled oceanographers to draw models of current flow free of the need to observe actual current movements. The method was popularized by German scientist Georg Wüst in 1924 when he calculated movements in the Florida Current and compared them with direct measurements made 40 years earlier by John Elliott Pillsbury for the United States government; the two sets of figures were convincingly similar.

The geostrophic method also enabled scientists to refine the types of measurements they required for their calculations and thus be more specific in their requests for information from oceanographers aboard research vessels. Soon oceanographers were measuring and documenting current circulation in far greater detail than previously had been possible. Current gyres were mapped in every ocean. In addition to the two primary gyres in the Atlantic Ocean, one moving clockwise in the North Atlantic, the other turning counterclockwise in the South Atlantic, a similar but larger pair swirled in the North and South Pacific as did a smaller set in the Indian Ocean, whose northern gyre changes with the seasonal monsoons.

While the revolving gyres explained much about current flow, a central mystery remained. Since the 19th Century, scientists and mariners had observed that currents along the west boundary of the gyres flowed faster than the currents to the east of the gyres. No creditable explanation for this intensification of western currents was advanced until 1947, when an eager young oceanographer named Henry Stommel, working at Woods Hole Oceanographic Institution, almost casually produced the answer. While driving to Providence, Rhode Island, with a colleague from Woods Hole, Raymond Montgomery, Stommel asked for suggestions as to areas of research. Montgomery mentioned the persistent and important problem of why the Gulf Stream was narrow and fast along the western boundary of the Atlantic Ocean. "Stommel," Montgomery noted years later, "answered the question qualitatively on a scrap of paper during a few minutes of discussion at a coffee stop during our short trip."

Stommel reasoned that the hub of each gyre is deflected to the west of the center of the gyre by the eastward rotation of the earth. As a result, a diffuse current along the eastern boundary moves in a broad, slow flow toward the Equator, typified by such currents as the California and Canaries.

Water thus conveyed to the Equator then travels west along either the North or the South Equatorial Current, backed by the persistent push of the trade winds. (A slow, narrow countercurrent flowing east in the region of the almost windless doldrums separates the North and South Equatorial Currents.) Where the Equatorial Current meets a land mass, it veers poleward. Because water speeds up in a narrow passage, this flow between the gyre's off-center hub and land creates a deep, swift westward boundary current and accounts for the powerful, high-speed flows of the Gulf Stream

THE GLOBAL PATTERN OF THE GYRES

The translation of energy from prevailing winds into the great current gyres that stir the world's oceans is an indirect process, affected by the spinning of the earth and by the continental barriers that divide ocean from ocean.

The major wind systems that power the surface gyres are the easterly trade winds, at about 15° north and south of the Equator, and prevailing westerlies at about 45° north and south latitude. Because of an effect of the earth's rotation these winds do not move water directly to the east or west, but nudge it to the right of the wind in the Northern Hemisphere, to the left in the Southern. The result is an accumulation of water between the wind belts, in low bulges that rise several feet above average sea level, centered at about 30° north or south latitude within each ocean gyre.

Gravity pulls the water downhill, away from the center of each bulge. But again the Coriolis effect asserts itself, deflecting the flow so that the current circles the hill, paralleling its contours.

The center of the current gyre, in another consequence of the earth's rotation, is offset toward the western edge of the ocean basin that confines it. The volume of water coursing poleward along the narrow western leg of the gyre, between the summit of the bulge and the adjacent continent, is the same as that circulating back toward the Equator down the broad eastern expanse. The constricted western currents thus are forced to flow faster and deeper than their eastern counterparts. The results are such powerful flows as the Gulf Stream, in the western North Atlantic, and the Kuroshio, in the North Pacific.

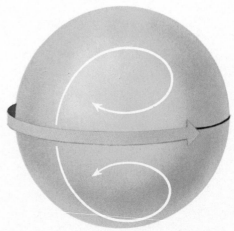

The rotation of the earth twists surface currents into gyres (*above*) that spin clockwise in the Northern Hemisphere, counterclockwise in the Southern. The earth's spin also deflects a gyre's central bulge to the west (*below*), constricting and intensifying the western current.

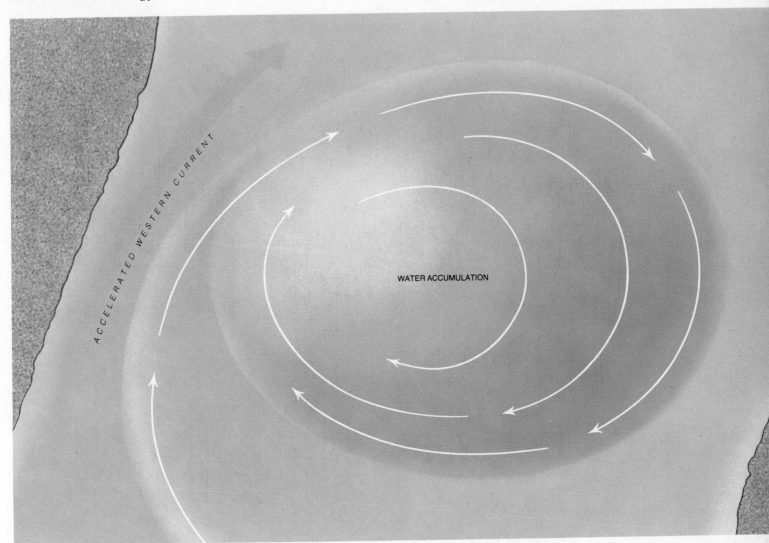

ACCELERATED WESTERN CURRENT

WATER ACCUMULATION

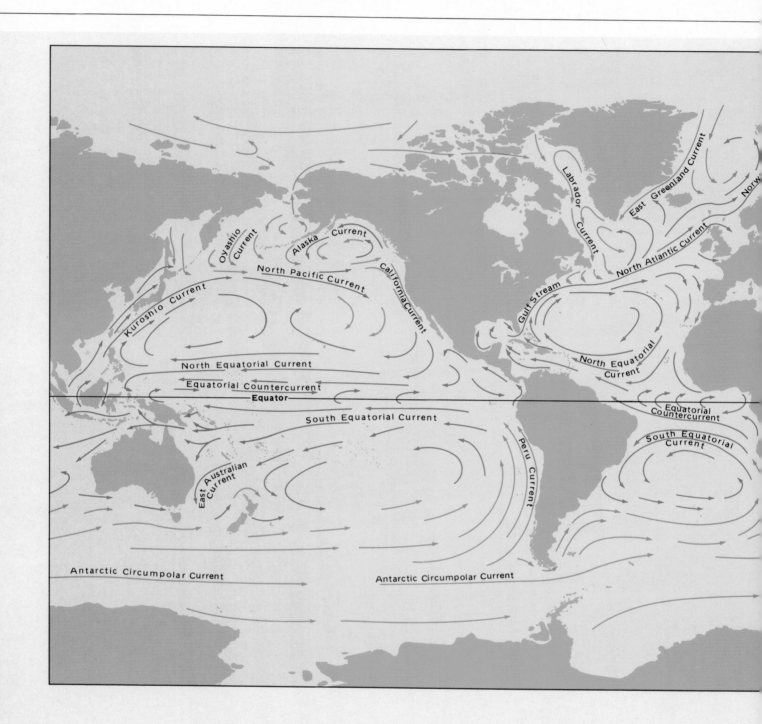

A pattern of interconnected gyres dominates a global map of ocean
surface currents. In the course of their ceaseless voyages, the wheeling
currents moderate world climate by exchanging tropical *(red)* and
polar *(blue)* water and circulate the nutrients essential for ocean life.

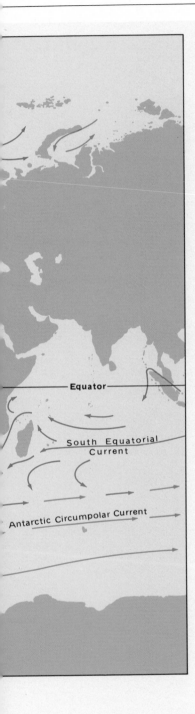

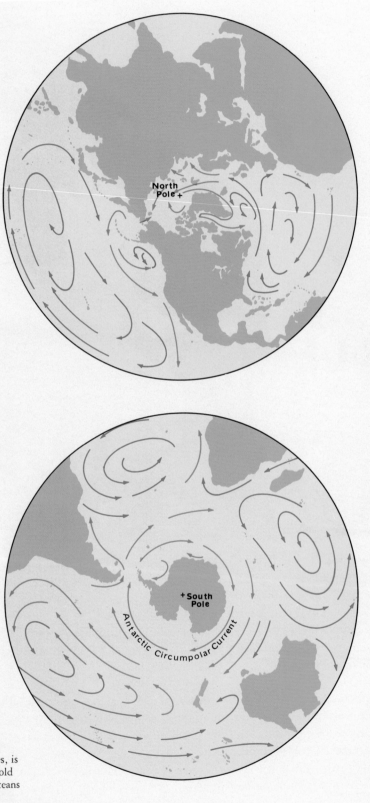

The largest current, and the only one unimpeded by land masses, is the Antarctic Circumpolar Current *(bottom right)*, which feeds cold polar water into the gyres of the Atlantic, Pacific and Indian Oceans as it circles the globe. In the Arctic Ocean *(top right)*, a trickle of water carried poleward through the Bering Strait from the North Pacific gyre mixes with water from North Atlantic currents.

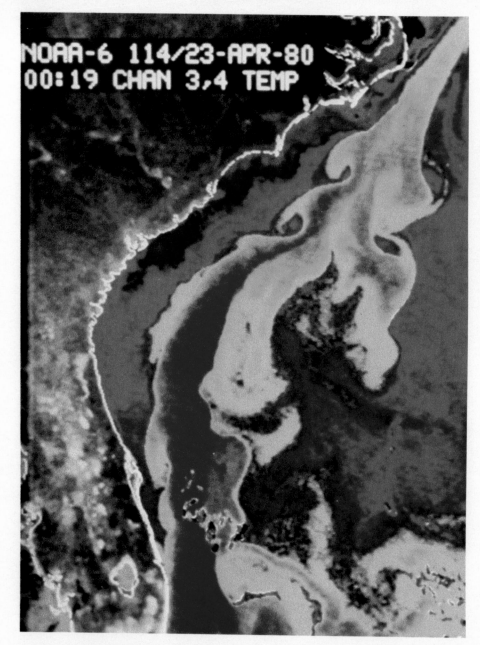

NOAA-6 114/23-APR-80 00:19 CHAN 3,4 TEMP

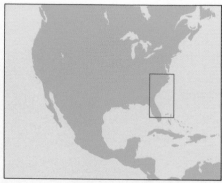

The convoluted Gulf Stream swirls past the southeast coast *(inset, above)* in this 1980 portrait *(left)* made by a heat-sensing radiometer aboard a U.S. National Oceanic and Atmospheric Administration satellite. The stream's warmest areas, which reach 84° F., appear as red in the computer-created image.

and the Japan Current, or Kuroshio. Thus water in the North Atlantic gyre might take a year to complete its circuit but would speed through portions of the Gulf Stream at 100 miles a day.

Stommel's paper explaining westward intensification, his first in the field, became a classic of clarity and simplicity in modern physical oceanography. It was an altogether fitting introduction to a career marked by profound contributions to the science.

Once technology provided the means to clock and measure the Gulf Stream, to take its temperature and photograph it from space, traditional conceptions were swiftly revised. The popular view of the current in the 19th Century had been succinctly expressed by Matthew Fontaine Maury, the famous compiler of *Wind and Current Charts*. His best-selling book, *The Physical Geography of the Sea*, included the compelling passage: "There is a river in the ocean: in the severest droughts it never fails, and in the mightiest floods, it never overflows; its banks and its bottom are of cold water, while its current is of warm; the Gulf of Mexico is its fountain and its mouth is in the Arctic Seas. It is the Gulf Stream."

Sinuous ribbons of water mark differences in density along the edge of the rapidly moving Gulf Stream as it passes through the Straits of Florida. The streaks appear where denser water is sinking beneath the stream's lighter flow.

It is a dramatic, inviting image but one that greater knowledge has proved to be almost entirely wrong. Contrary to Maury's calculations and assumptions, the Gulf Stream is not born in the Gulf of Mexico, is not bounded by colder water on both sides and does not empty into the Arctic Sea. Indeed, the Gulf Stream is not even a river, but a far more complex network of ocean currents, more properly called the Gulf Stream System, that constantly change course and even split into separate, circling currents meandering about the Atlantic.

Still, the Gulf Stream is an entity bounded by sharp lines of demarcation that often can be seen and measured, especially on its north side, as surely as if it were a river. In the process of attempting to solve its many mysteries, oceanographers have found the stream to be a source of fascination and not a little controversy.

Popular misconceptions about the source of the Gulf Stream collapsed quickly under scientific scrutiny. Early explorers had suggested that the outflow of the Mississippi River fed the current, yet the Gulf Stream's transport — as oceanographers call the amount of water in its flow — proved to be 1,000 times that of the Mississippi. Moreover, belying its name, the Gulf Stream was found to receive little of its water from the Gulf of Mexico. In fact, the waters that make up the stream first travel all the way across the Atlantic.

Pushed by the trade winds, the westward-flowing South Equatorial Current is split in two by the projecting bulge of Brazil. As the fragment that is deflected northward moves up the South American coast and across the Equator, it is joined by the full force of the North Equatorial Current. The blended currents are soon split once again into tributaries; the largest branch moves seaward of the Antilles islands in the Caribbean Sea; another filters through the islands of the Caribbean, rushes through the Yucatan Channel into the Gulf of Mexico, then speeds through the Straits of Florida into the Atlantic. It is the speed of this fast-moving mass of water that helps to power the Gulf Stream on its great transatlantic course.

In the corridor between Florida and the Bahamas, as narrow as 50 miles across and 2,600 feet deep, the crowded water races at up to 10 miles per hour, faster than any other current in the Atlantic. The Florida Current carries one billion cubic feet of water past Miami, Florida, every second. Just north of the Bahama Islands, where the Antilles Current joins the Florida Current, the Gulf Stream System expands to more than three times the size of the Florida Current as it funneled through the Straits; the system then begins to slow as it approaches Cape Hatteras and starts its dramatic turn out into the Atlantic.

Exactly why the current veers eastward at this point is unknown, although it has been suggested that the stream merely follows a great circle route while the coastline turns back to the north. At any rate, the current continues into the Atlantic until it passes south of the Grand Banks. Its northern line of demarcation is often clear and sharp. So abrupt is the change from the colder water to warmer water in the stream — the temperature rises as much as 18° F. in 10 miles — that some oceanographers call the northern boundary of the current the "cold wall." (The colder water north of this wall is called slope water because it lies over the continental slope.) The stream in this path from Cape Hatteras to the Grand Banks is at its fullest volume, sweeping five billion cubic feet of water per second northeastward into the ocean at three to four miles per hour.

Yet even along its sharply delineated northern boundary the Gulf Stream is no river. According to shipboard observations by Woods Hole oceanographer Frederick C. Fuglister in the 1950s, its warmest water is scattered through the stream in bands, which alternate with ribbons of cool water. The stream's speed varies in similar alternating bands that constantly shift courses. Many a skipper, believing he was taking advantage of the stream, has found a faster current carrying another vessel past him only a mile or so away. The stream's boundaries fluctuate continually, but without altering its overall northeastern course.

Rolling on eastward into the North Atlantic, still touching bottom nearly a mile down, its speed finally reduced to one to two miles per hour, the Gulf Stream approaches the Grand Banks off the New England coast. Here it is met by another big stream, the Labrador Current, bringing icy water down from the Hudson Bay and Greenland. For a few miles the two currents flow side by side in opposite directions so close to each other that the bow of a ship crossing the currents may enter one stream while the stern is in the other. Crewmen aboard a U.S. Coast Guard frigate that encountered just such a situation recorded a difference of 22° F. between the water temperatures at the vessel's bow and stern.

As the two great currents converge, part of the cold Labrador water sinks beneath the stream's warm water and flows along the bottom, which drops precipitously beyond the Grand Banks. The cold subsurface Labrador water moves on southward, some of it mingling with the Gulf Stream waters above, gradually cooling the stream and slowing its speed.

Nominally, the Gulf Stream ends here; oceanographers refer to its continuation as the North Atlantic Current. Part of this current makes a slow turn toward the south, sweeping down in the final leg of the North Atlantic gyre to join the Canaries Current off Europe and the North Equatorial Current that originally brought these warm waters up the Florida coast. There, its waters are heated again by the tropical sun and speeded by the trade winds on its way westward across the Atlantic to complete its perpetual circle.

The northerly waters of the Gulf Stream retain some of the warmth absorbed along the Equator. The continuation of this current, the North Atlantic Current, sweeps northeastward past the British Isles, moving much more slowly; its speed is a fraction of that of the Gulf Stream as it approaches Northern Europe. The North Atlantic Current in fact is no longer much of a current; it spreads out into a fan with a series of tributaries that

Scuba divers inspect the 48-foot submersible, *Ben Franklin*, designed by explorer-scientist Jacques Piccard to drift within the Gulf Stream. During a 30-day, 1,500-mile voyage in 1969, Piccard and his crew detected a number of powerful subsurface eddies, one of which carried the *Franklin* far off course.

go off in many directions. One branch curves up past Iceland, turning west and south along Greenland. Another branch reaches all the way into the Arctic Sea, where Maury thought all of the Gulf Stream emptied.

After World War II, improvements in technology permitted scientists to refine the geography of the Gulf Stream—and presented them with a surprise. In the late 1940s, Fuglister of Woods Hole, studying surface currents and subsurface temperature and salinity profiles, found indications of a curious phenomenon: Large circles of water break away from the Gulf Stream and whirl off on their own. In 1950, Fuglister led a six-vessel expedition known as Operation *Cabot* to search for these oddities. For three weeks Operation *Cabot* crisscrossed the Gulf Stream, studying the shifting bands of currents within the main current. The scientists succeeded in identifying an eddy that had separated from the Gulf Stream and proceeded in nearly the opposite direction, revolving like a miniature ocean gyre.

Further investigation disclosed a series of "meanders"—narrow bulges that protruded now and again from the stream's edge. Some of them were

Scientists aboard the research ship *Knorr* launch a free-floating buoy to be tracked by satellite during a 1977 study of Gulf Stream eddies. One such buoy was released in April, about 200 miles off the coast of Cape Hatteras, North Carolina, in a strong eddy dubbed Ring Bob *(map, opposite).*

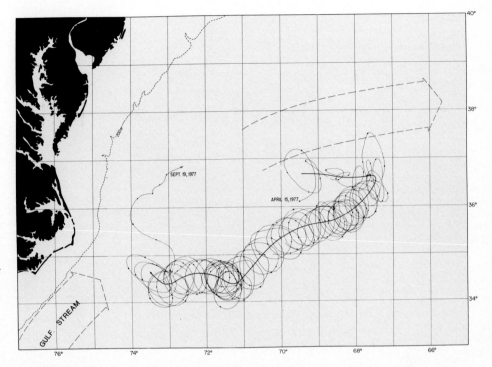

The surprising five-month journey of the *Knorr's* buoy and Ring Bob is shown on this map. The eddy briefly traveled east with the Gulf Stream, as might be expected, but then veered sharply southwest, covering about three miles a day through the Sargasso Sea before rejoining the stream and dissipating in mid-September.

drawn back into the mainstream of the current. But others broke away, forming rings that spun in counterclockwise circles and moved westward through the Atlantic. By 1975, scientists using a buoy that could be tracked by an orbiting satellite found that nearly a dozen meanders occur every year. In 1977, Philip L. Richardson and fellow Woods Hole oceanographers went out to examine one as it developed.

A tracking buoy had picked up a meander that had just broken away from the southern edge of the Gulf Stream's main flow. Richardson and his associates named it Ring Bob and set out after it in the research vessel *Knorr*. Plotting its course from the satellite data, they moved to intercept the ring and as soon as they entered the errant current, as Richardson wrote, "we could see, feel and smell the presence of the ring's Slope Water core from the deck of the ship." Ring Bob was composed largely of cold slope water from just beyond the north edge of the Gulf Stream, encompassed by a ring of warm Gulf Stream water, some 50 miles in diameter, swirling around the cold core. "Immediately on entering the central part," Richardson continued, "we noticed a seaweed smell, similar to that of a seashore on a summer day. The water was obviously green and turbid as compared to the clear and deep blue of the nearby Gulf Stream and the Sargasso Sea. The temperature of the surface water in the center was 39° F., nearly 9° F. colder than the surrounding water; this difference was reflected in the air temperature."

Richardson and his colleagues, plotting Bob's course by satellite and revisiting it during the succeeding months, were able to assemble a portrait of the ring "covering all stages of Bob's life, from birth to death."

It was a remarkable life. After starting to form as a meander in February 1977 and whirling off on its own in March, Bob had circled back toward the stream again in April, had attached itself and traveled next to the Gulf Stream but in the opposite direction for a month, and then had spun away on its own again in May. Not until September did it meet its parent current

The formation of the eddy known as Ring Bob began in February of 1977. A map based on data received from a heat-sensing satellite shows a pronounced southward meander in the warm current of the Gulf Stream.

Eight days after the meander originated, its loop tightens, drawing cold, nutrient-rich slope water, which is normally found over the slope of the continental shelf, into a pocket in the warm Sargasso Sea.

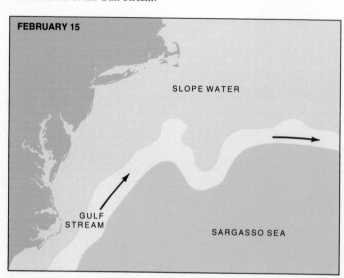

FEBRUARY 15

SLOPE WATER

GULF STREAM

SARGASSO SEA

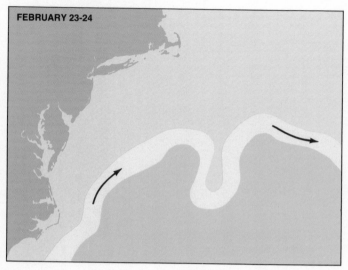

FEBRUARY 23-24

again, off the Chesapeake Bay. The Gulf Stream enfolded Ring Bob, dissipated its rotating motion and moved on as it had before.

Richardson had meanwhile studied Ring Bob's speed (roughly three miles per hour) and its changing temperatures and salinities at various depths all the way to the bottom of the Atlantic. And while concentrating on Bob, they and other oceanographers were at the same time keeping a satellite watch on half a dozen similar rings north and south of the stream.

Extrapolating from these findings and using Fuglister's work as a basis, Richardson and the other ring experts worked out a rough anatomy of the fluctuating stream. As it moves northeastward after leaving Cape Hatteras, its bands of warm and cold water diverge, converge and collide, giving the stream an erratic path. Occasionally the path will dip southward or rise northward in a meander so pronounced that its sides meet, forming a loop. A loop extending the northern edge of the stream enfolds a core of warm Sargasso Sea water, while a loop protruding south contains cold slope water. The loop itself spins in its own circulatory current. This self-contained whirlpool then pinches off and breaks away from the stream, moving back westward at about three miles per day.

What causes the break remains a mystery. The fact that the Gulf Stream's current persists all the way to the sea bottom may be a factor; the sloping continental shelf and a succession of peaks called the New England Seamounts could set up a swirling motion that would send a section of the stream off its course.

But other puzzles remain, despite masses of accumulated evidence and millions of computer calculations. Why are the southern rings larger than the northern rings? The former can spread across a stretch of ocean as large as half of New England. They are deeper, and they survive longer — an average of one and one half years and as much as three years — before being absorbed again by the Gulf Stream. The normal northern ring is smaller and shallower and rarely survives longer than three months. One explanation offered for its shorter existence is geographical: Since it spins off north of the stream and heads back toward the continent, it is trapped between the stream and the coastline, and the coastal countercurrent sweeps it back into the Gulf Stream.

In another two days, the meander's loop closes completely, trapping a core of cold water within a swirling ring of warm Gulf Stream water. The movement of this warm water imparts a counterclockwise spin to the ring.

Within two weeks, Ring Bob has broken free of the Gulf Stream to begin its independent journey through the Atlantic Ocean, spinning in the direction opposite to that of the warm current that formed it.

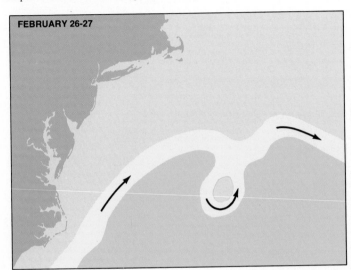

FEBRUARY 26-27

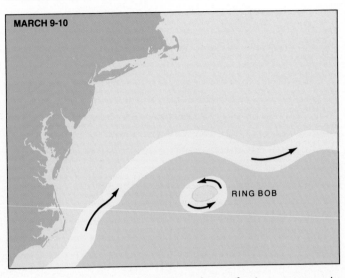

MARCH 9-10

RING BOB

Meanders and rings almost surely occur at the edges of other currents in other oceans. Oceanographer William R. Holland theorizes that meanders and rings provide a braking effect without which the Gulf Stream might continue to accelerate until the current would begin to break up. Recent findings also indicate that eddies speed the recirculation of deeper waters and increase the amount of water transported in the stream. According to Philip Richardson, five times as much volume is carried by the current as a result of the mixing action of the eddies.

The concept of rings has contributed substantially to the understanding of the Gulf Stream, yet Stommel contends that oceanographers know just enough about the current to realize how little they know. Even though indisputable evidence exists that heat is transported northward in the Gulf Stream, no one knows exactly how it happens. In Stommel's words, "The structure in that portion of the Atlantic is so complicated that we hardly know how to speak of heat transport of the Gulf Stream." In terms of scientific proof, he insists that "we really don't know whether there's any heat flow northward in the ocean at all."

But in his most striking conclusion Stommel sought to eradicate the misleading concept that the stream behaves like a river in the ocean. The image of a river suggests a single current that flows through surrounding waters yet is distinct from them. The stream, according to Stommel, is more accurately envisioned as the swiftly moving western boundary of the warm Sargasso Sea, whose edge can be most clearly discerned where it meets the cold water to the north. Properly understood, Stommel said, "the Gulf Stream is not a warm river but a wall between hot and cold water. The Gulf Stream 'exists' as a physical entity in the same sense as the boundary layer next to an aerofoil exists." Thus the stream continues to be the mariner's marvel and the oceanographer's challenge, serving as a massive dividing line between the northern Atlantic and its warm southern center.

That center, the Sargasso Sea, is an ocean wonder in itself. Locked within the North Atlantic gyre, it revolves in slow motion like the hub of a giant wheel, the rim of which is composed of the Gulf Stream System, the North Atlantic, the Canaries and North Equatorial Currents. The perpetually sun-warmed sea is highly saline because of evaporation and little diluting rainfall. With no upwelling to bring nutrients from the deep to cloud the water, the sea is nearly as clear as if it were distilled. Some of the oceans' oddest flora and fauna have adapted to its peculiarities, most notably, huge tracts of sargasso weed.

Some of the earliest Greek maps indicate masses of seaweed in the Atlantic. No doubt Phoenician, Arabian and Portuguese mariners brushed the easternmost edges of the Sargasso Sea; and a chart drawn by Andrea Bianca in 1436 included what he labeled as Mer de Baga — Sea of Berries — in the mid-Atlantic. Portuguese sailors named the weed after an herb native to Portugal.

The weed itself is the most striking feature of the Sargasso Sea; it floats in meadows of small, yellow-brown, feathery clumps across an area of the North Atlantic nearly the size of the continental United States. It was thought at first to be coastal seaweed that had been torn from its rocks by storms and carried over thousands of miles and years into the core of the North Atlantic gyre. But later oceanographers realized that all the shores of the North Atlantic could not provide enough weed to account for the millions of tons of it that float in the Sargasso Sea.

The sargasso weed's ancestors probably did come from the coasts of the Atlantic; it still bears a resemblance to rockweed. But ensnared by the converging waters of the North Atlantic gyre, it has evolved into two distinct species, *Sargassum natans* and *Sargassum fluitans,* neither of which retains the holdfasts with which coastal weed clings to the rocks. Clusters of pea-sized gas bladders keep the weed afloat on the surface of the Sargasso Sea.

Sargasso weed — vegetation drifting in the slow circle of the sea's largest internal eddy — is thus the sea's largest example of phytoplankton. For all its immense volume, it generally appears to be sparsely scattered over the water. For centuries seafarers told tales of ships caught in the drifting tangle of weed, but no such derelicts have ever been found. Some of this legend can be attributed to the calms and doldrums common at that latitude. The sargasso weed itself forms only clumps on the surface, too thin even to foul a propeller.

Because it shelters more than it feeds the zooplankton and fish of the Sargasso Sea, the weed can live for centuries; some botanists estimate that there are sargasso weeds floating in the Sea that were there when Columbus passed through. But even sargasso weed is mortal. Gradually an ancient patch of it loses some of its gas bladders. Bryozoans, minute invertebrates called moss animals, attach themselves to the fronds of the weed; and as this parasite grows, its weight drags the sargassum beneath the surface. Eventually these ancient patches of weed, white-pocked and burdened with bryozoan growth, sink beneath the reach of the nurturing sunlight, die and drift on downward to add their own nutrients to the rich, cold waters underneath the Sea.

During its lifetime, the weed shields a wide variety of marine fauna adapted for survival among its sheltering fronds. Perhaps the most remarkable of the creatures that inhabit the Sargasso Sea is the common European eel. The life cycle of *Anguilla anguilla* was a puzzle to Aristotle, who was one of the first to observe mature fresh-water eels going out to sea and young elvers returning to the rivers from the ocean. But where did the adult eels breed? And how did they breed at all? They appeared to have no reproductive organs. The mystery began to unravel in 1856, when a German naturalist discovered a flat, nearly transparent sea creature that resembled the leaf of a willow tree. He named it leptocephalus, meaning in Greek "slender-head." At the turn of the century, two Italian ichthyologists, who were keeping some specimens of leptocephalus in their aquarium, were astonished to find their transparent flatfish metamorphosing into young eels.

With the identification of the eels' larval stage, the search could begin for their spawning ground. Johannes Schmidt, a Danish oceanographer-ichthyologist, caught a few leptocephali west of Denmark's Faeroe Islands. Recognizing the primary stage of the European eel, he decided to see how far west in the Atlantic he could find the tiny flatfish.

It took him 18 years. Crisscrossing the Atlantic in fishing vessels, carefully plotting the location of every leptocephalus brought up in his fine-mesh nets, and moving steadily westward toward the North American coast, Schmidt made the important discovery that the farther west he went, the smaller were the leptocephali. Clearly he was closing in on their place of birth. Finally in 1922, he brought up the smallest specimen of all — three tenths of an inch long. The spot where he found it was 600 miles southeast of Bermuda, in the midst of the Sargasso Sea.

Now that scientists knew where to look, they found transparent, pea-sized anguilla eggs 500 feet down in Sargasso waters. Since then, ichthyologists, including Schmidt, have tracked leptocephali back across the Atlantic and have filled in most of the gaps in the eel's life cycle. The opposite of the anadromous salmon, a salt-water fish that breeds in fresh water, the European common eel is catadromous, a fresh-water fish that spawns in salt water.

Swimming near the bottom at five to 10 miles per day, millions of mature eels, seven to 14 years old, leave the rivers of Europe for their distant spawning grounds in the Sargasso Sea. The females are about three feet long, the males half that size. Their exact route is still unknown. They may follow the Canaries Current into the North Equatorial Current. But at the depth they apparently travel, the effect of the currents could be minimized, and the eels may swim directly across the Atlantic. As they move westward, their reproductive organs mature; the eels' color changes from yellow-green to metallic silver, with a band of black along the top. Their skin toughens; their nostrils dilate and their eyes enlarge. The purple retina of their eyes, best adapted to blue-green light in fresh water, alters to a golden color that better absorbs the blue light of deep sea water. They cease feeding; they have amassed enough fat for the entire journey. Their teeth fall out and their digestive tracts atrophy. They become little more than carriers of eggs and milt.

Somewhere 3,000 miles from Europe's rivers and deep in the Sargasso Sea — no one knows exactly where — the females deposit their eggs. Some ichthyologists hypothesize that the female's eggs are forced out by the water pressure at great depth. The males' milt fertilizes the eggs. And both males and females, their mission accomplished, die in the Sargasso Sea. Now begins the even more remarkable migration of their progeny.

The leaflike leptocephali, only a quarter of an inch long, gently float toward the surface of the Sargasso Sea. There they drift — their transparency offering some protection from predators — until in the slow circuit of the

Hardly the treacherous, weed-choked
graveyard of ships portrayed in seafaring legend,
the Sargasso Sea, dotted with patches of
sargasso weed, lies at the calm center of the
North Atlantic Current gyre.

A clump of sargasso weed floats in the tranquil waters of the Sargasso Sea, a two-million-square-mile area of the western North Atlantic that is characterized by immense amounts of this unique seaweed. Myriad tiny creatures such as the crab at right have been taking refuge in the sargassum for so long that they have evolved a camouflage identical to the weed.

Sargasso they reach the fringe of the Gulf Stream. Riding the stream, they are carried toward Europe at a rate that takes as long as three years.

They still are leptocephali. Not until they approach the European shores does the imprint of their inborn senses trigger their move into the fresh waters draining from the rivers into the Atlantic. Whether, like salmon, they return to the same rivers their parents left is not known. But as they move toward the rivers, they undergo the metamorphosis that so long baffled the ichthyologists. The flat body, by this time about three inches long, elongates, becomes tubular, and lengthens to a foot or more. The leptocephali have transformed into young anguilla by the time they swim up the rivers of Europe.

Meanwhile, a somewhat similar migratory-and-spawning phenomenon occurs off the American coast. A slightly different species of American anguilla swims out across the Gulf Stream into the Sargasso Sea to give birth to leptocephali that return to American rivers. Their spawning ground is as much a mystery as that of the European species. But ichthyologists know that they are separate. Presumably the American eel larvae are born at the southern edge of the Sargasso Sea, to be carried to the American coast by the North Equatorial Current.

One American icthyologist, D. W. Tucker, theorizes that perhaps these eels' progeny never return to their parents' rivers but join the eastward migration of their European cousins in the Gulf Stream. This theory suggests that most of the European eels never complete the long voyage to the Sargasso Sea, and that all the European elvers are of American origin.

In a fascinating adaptation to circumstance, the larval stage of the American eel, which has far less distance to travel than the European eel, is significantly briefer than that of its European relative. Thus a masterwork of timing triggers its metamorphosis into a fresh-water eel precisely as it approaches the American coast.

While painstaking research has provided answers to many of the mysteries surrounding the life cycle of the eel, scientists have yet to isolate the biological imperative that propels one group of eel larvae to the current that will carry it to Europe and the other group to the current heading toward North America. Ω

SCANNING THE SEAS FROM SPACE

Oceanographers have long been hampered by the vastness of their subject: Until recently, collecting data from a significant area of ocean required many costly and time-consuming voyages by specially equipped ships. But satellite sensors, circling the earth every few hours at altitudes of 500 miles or more, can swiftly survey huge expanses.

One instrument frequently used in weather satellites gauges the amount of infrared or microwave energy radiated from the water — providing a clue to sea-surface temperatures, and thus to patterns of currents. Another device, orbiting aboard the weather satellite Nimbus 7, is sensitive to reflected energy in wavelengths that indicate the presence of chlorophyll — the characteristic pigment of green plants and a sign of abundant marine life.

The first satellite designed solely for oceanographic research, Seasat, carried an instrument that probed the sea surface with radar. Called a scatterometer, the device gauged the amount of radio emissions scattered by wind-generated waves and derived a useful measure of wind speed at the sea surface. Another of Seasat's instruments, a radar altimeter, revealed wave heights and also the subtle contours of the overall sea surface.

Satellite sensors still have their limitations. They cannot probe beneath the waves, for example, and the computer-generated images on these and the following pages depict only surface-water properties. Nevertheless, says Dr. Robert Bernstein of the Scripps Institution, "Where once the crucial place for an oceanographer was on a ship at sea, soon it may be onshore in front of a computer system monitoring data from satellites passing overhead."

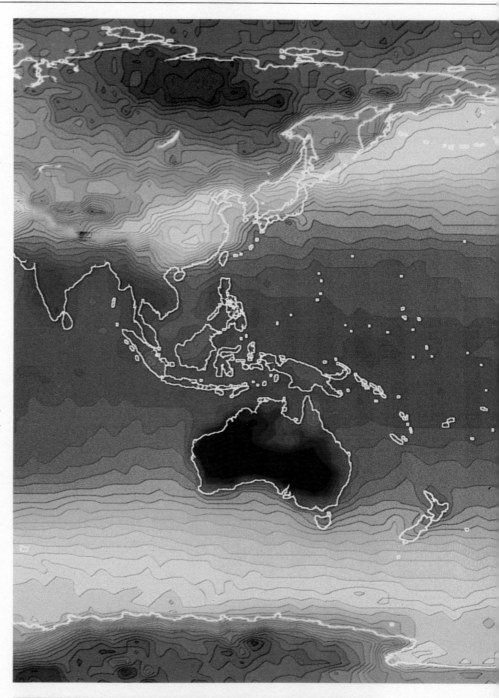

The path traced by Seasat during three days in 1978 shows how the tilt of its orbit, combined with the rotation of the globe, brought most of the world's seas within range of its sensors. Gaps in the tracing indicate interrupted or garbled transmissions.

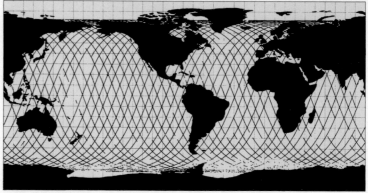

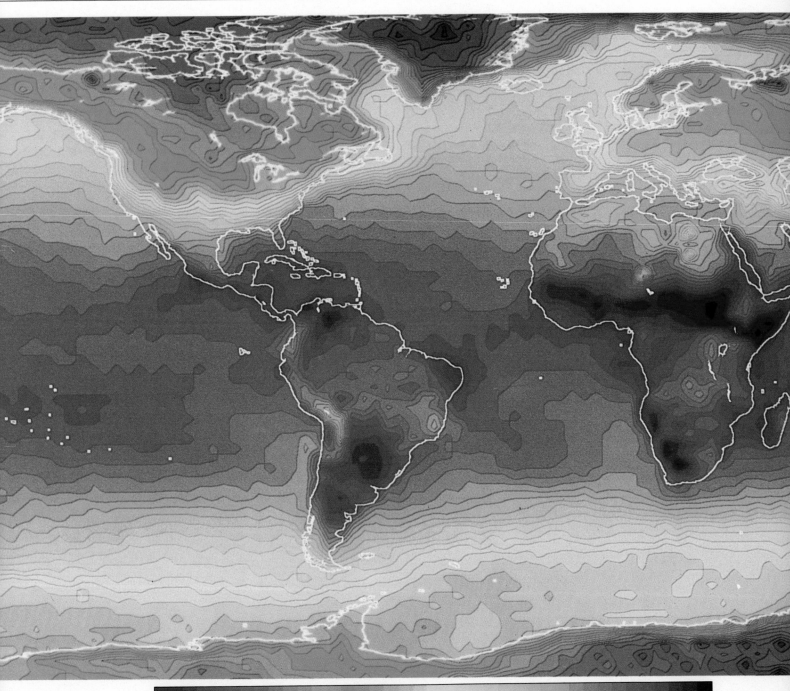

Degrees Kelvin 243 253 263 273 283 293 303 313

Derived from satellite readings of infrared
and microwave radiation, the map above charts
global average sea- and land-surface
temperatures during January 1979. Each
increment on the scale below the map
indicates a temperature change of 2° Kelvin or
3.6° F.; water freezes at 273° Kelvin.

A computer-tinted rendition of data from the Nimbus 7 satellite reveals variations in chlorophyll content in the North Atlantic. Red-orange indicates a high concentration of marine plant life; the blue of eddying Gulf Stream waters betrays their infertility.

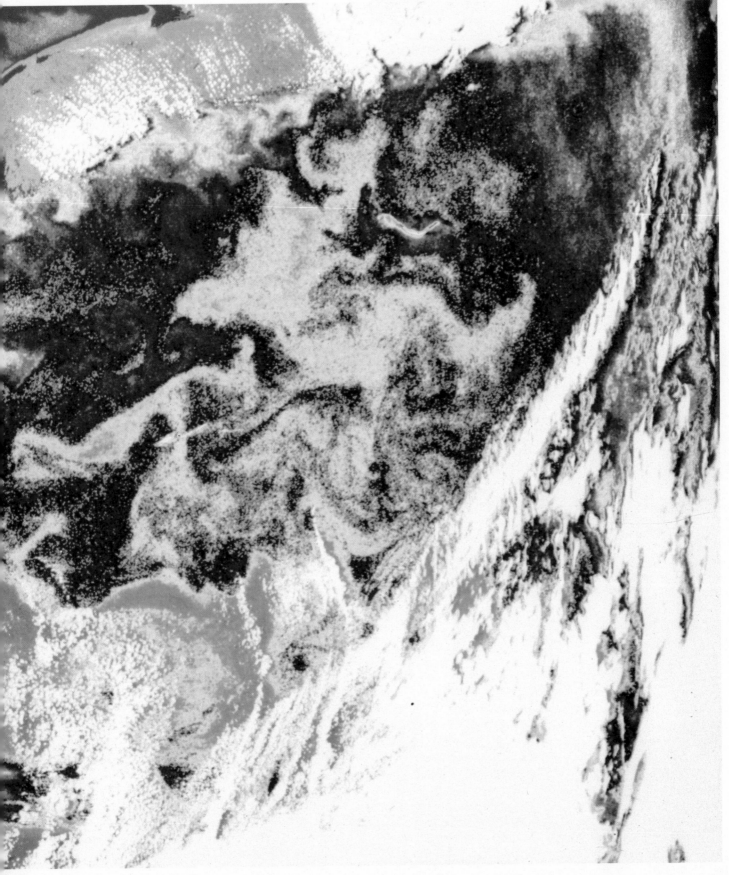

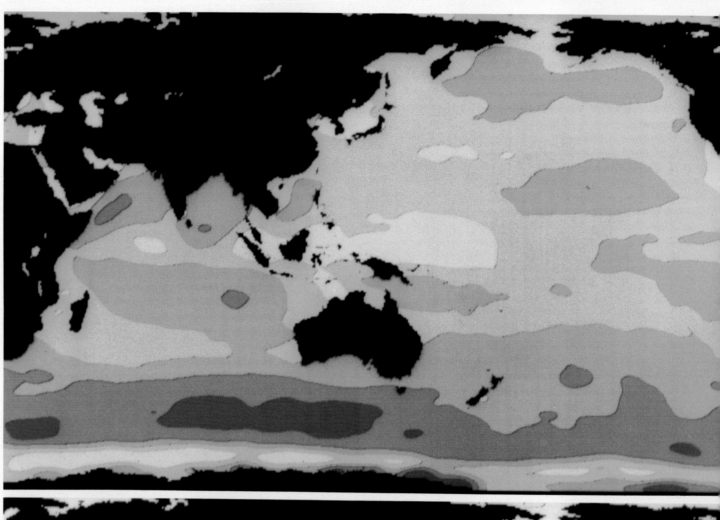

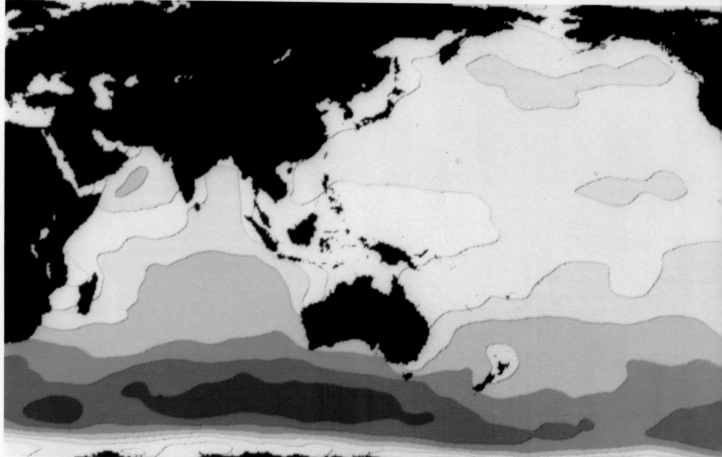

68

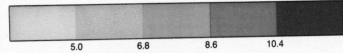

5.0   6.8   8.6   10.4

Compiled from Seasat's radar measurements of sea-surface chop, this map charts surface wind speeds as averaged from July to October 1978. The depicted speeds range from less than 11 mph (*yellow*) to more than 23 mph (*brown*).

Meters

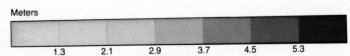

1.3   2.1   2.9   3.7   4.5   5.3

This global map of average wave conditions embodies altimeter data collected by Seasat between July and October 1978. Depending on the strength and persistence of the winds, the wave heights range from less than four feet (*lilac*) to more than 17 feet (*indigo*).

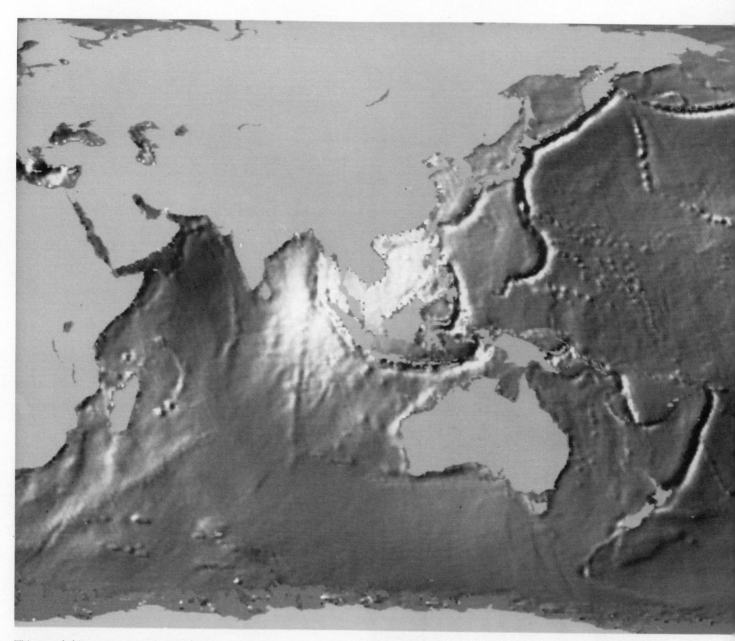

This remarkable computer image of the surface of the world's oceans *(above)* was produced in 1982 from analysis of altimeter data collected four years earlier by Seasat. The computer-generated colors of the sea surface indicate the amount of slope (in meters per degree of longitude, as shown in the key at far right) and mirror the topography of the sea floor. As diagramed at right, a slight increase in gravity over submarine concentrations of mass, such as midocean ridges, draws water away from undersea trenches, where gravity is less; the resulting differences in the elevation of the water can be as great as 60 feet.

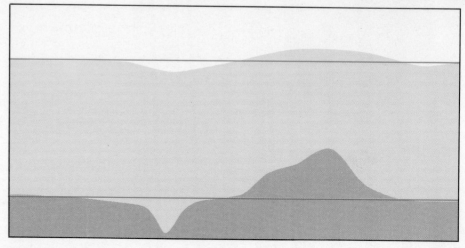

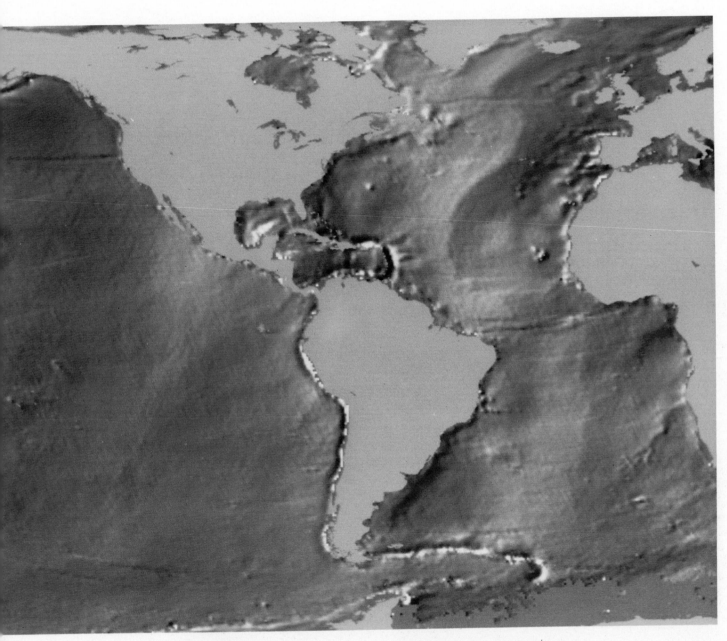

NW-SE Gradient
Meters/Degree

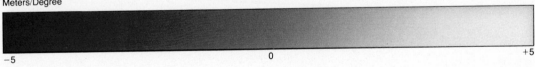

−5   0   +5

Chapter 3

A PARTNERSHIP OF WIND AND WATER

In June of 1982, meteorologists noted a sudden and dramatic drop in atmospheric pressure at two widely separated points in the southeastern Pacific, Tahiti and Easter Island. About a month later, weather stations on Fanning and Christmas Islands in the mid-Pacific reported an unusual rise in sea level, of six to 10 inches. At the same time, the sea level at Palau and Guadalcanal in the western Pacific dropped four to six inches. Growing suspicions that something strange was happening, on a very large scale, were soon confirmed. Water temperatures in the ocean near the Equator began to rise, gradually but persistently. Off the coast of Peru, temperatures reached 80° F. — twelve degrees above normal. In the mid-Pacific, temperatures reached 86° F., nine degrees higher than normal, a level that one scientist called "about as hot as the ocean can get."

By late summer, a meteorological tragedy was in the making: Indonesia was in the grip of a widespread and devastating drought. With crops shriveled in the sun, a million people faced famine; hundreds were already dead of starvation. In Australia, a relentless heat wave and drought transformed thousands of acres of farmland into desert. Savage winds swept up the sparse topsoil and whirled it into blinding dust storms. Bone-dry brush burst into flame and the ensuing conflagrations killed 72 people, leaving 8,000 homeless and destroying three billion dollars' worth of property. Across the Indian Ocean, Southern Africa was suffering the worst dry spell in history. Farm animals died by the tens of thousands, and scorched fields yielded but a fraction of their normal harvest. Subsequent disease and malnutrition tripled the human death rate. And still the drought spread — to India, Sri Lanka, the Philippines, Hawaii and Mexico.

At the same time, other parts of the world were experiencing catastrophic flooding. For eight months, coastal areas of Ecuador and Peru suffered torrential rains — in some cases 300 times normal annual rainfall — and the worst floods of the century. Tens of thousands of adobe dwellings simply dissolved in the downpours. Avalanches and swollen rivers isolated scores of towns; more than 300 people died. In the mid-Pacific, French Polynesia, which experiences a typhoon on the average of once every 50 years, was battered by five in as many months. Unusually warm ocean currents disrupted the fish population; Peru's multimillion-dollar anchovy industry was devastated, and on Christmas Island, 17 million birds disappeared without a trace when the fish they fed on moved away.

In December 1982, the meteorological mayhem moved into the United States. A dozen people died on the West Coast as high winds and relentless

A waterspout, first cousin of the tornado, dances off the Florida coast. Waterspouts occur in fair weather or foul, day or night, in warm climates or cold, and provide a dramatic demonstration of the constant, complex interaction between the ocean and its most intimate neighbor, the air.

rain chewed up beaches, brought homes and piers crashing down into the surf, and triggered mud slides that smothered crops and devoured much of California's magnificent coastal highway. A freak tornado cut a swath of destruction through downtown Los Angeles. Between December and the following April, damages in the Mountain and Pacific states totaled an estimated one billion dollars. Another billion dollars' worth of property and crops was destroyed along the U.S. Gulf Coast, where floods drove 60,000 people from their homes and killed 50. The same combination of events, one awed meteorologist predicted, "won't happen again in a couple hundred years."

Before the storms had run their course, scientists had deciphered a pattern in the disparate upheavals and had traced a convoluted skein of cause-and-effect relationships back to what appeared to be their source. The culprit, it turned out, was a warm current that had intruded into the coastal waters of Peru — an event that occurs so regularly, around Christmas time, that it has long been known by a colloquial Spanish term for the Christ child: *El Niño*. Once the concern only of the Peruvian fishermen whose catches were disrupted by its appearance, El Niño in 1982 had run amuck, precipitating a global catastrophe that one scientist called "the oceanographic event of the century."

Like many natural disasters, El Niño brought with its visitations of death and destruction a gift of knowledge. It provided scientists with an unprecedented opportunity to analyze the infinitely complex relationships between ocean currents and prevailing winds, between the mysterious behavior of enormous pools of warm water in the Pacific Ocean and equally perplexing changes in atmospheric pressure elsewhere, between the disappearance of the Christmas Island birds and the raging brush fires of Australia.

For centuries, Peruvian seafarers have reaped an abundant harvest of fish from their coastal waters. The bounty is found in a narrow tongue of cold, nutrient-rich water located in the midst of a cool current that flows northward along the coast of South America. Spanish conquistadors took advantage of the chilly waters to cool their wine, suspending it in flagons over the sides of their ships. In 1802 the German naturalist Alexander von Humboldt, for whom the current was named, recorded its temperature for the first time — water in the current is about two degrees cooler than its surroundings. He theorized, incorrectly, that the cool surface water was flowing northward from Antarctica (later studies showed that the Peru Current, as it is now called, originated in lower latitudes).

By the mid-19th Century, scientists had deduced that the coldest, richest water — the narrow tongue in which the fish were most numerous — was not coming from the current at all but was being drawn upward from below. The trade winds blowing almost constantly toward the northwest move surface water offshore, water that is replaced by cold water rising from far below. Such upwelling is found off the western coasts of all continents but is most vigorous and extensive off the coast of Peru because of the intensity of the trade winds there. This vertical circulation plays a vital role in ocean ecology by bringing nutrients that have settled toward the ocean floor back within reach of the fish that inhabit the upper levels of the water.

Along the northern edge of the Peru Current, where the upwelling is most pronounced, the sea teems with life. Naturalist Robert Cushman

Debris-filled water floods California's San Joaquin delta *(below)* after torrential downpours in December of 1982; and dust sifts across the drought-stricken plains of eastern Australia *(right)* in March of 1983. Both weather aberrations could be traced to the arrival off Peru some months before of a disastrous warm current called El Niño.

Murphy, sailing in his research schooner *Askoy* near the Galapagos Islands one night in the 1930s, encountered an abrupt line of demarcation between warm, comparatively barren waters to the north and the area of upwelling. Suddenly the night came alive. The sea was "seething, boiling with life," Murphy recalled. There were "small herring-like fishes, a silvery hatchet-fish with its face bitten off, rudder fishes, hanging head downward, luminous lanternfishes with shining light pores, red and purple swimming crabs, other creatures which we could not name at sight and much that was too small even to see distinctly."

Such is the profusion that normally exists in these waters. But at intervals of two to 10 years, the cool upwelling is supplanted by warm water from the north—El Niño. Deprived of the abundant plankton that thrive in the nutrient-rich water, the fish begin to die or migrate, as do the millions of birds that feed on the fish. Sometimes the death toll is so great that hydrogen sulfide released by the decaying bodies of fish and birds combines with sea fog to blacken boats and even cars and houses on shore. The intrusion of warm water also disrupts the normally cool, dry weather along the coast, bringing heat and moisture that cause torrential rain.

Even when El Niño extends no farther than Peruvian waters, it can have worldwide economic impact. After a prolonged appearance of the phenomenon in 1972, Peru's anchovy catch—normally one of the world's richest harvests of fish—was reduced by 80 per cent. The consequent shortage of fish meal, used as a commercial chicken feed in the United States, led to a rise in chicken prices for U.S. consumers. In addition, the birds that fed on the anchovies disappeared from the area, diminishing the world's supply of guano fertilizer, which is derived from dried sea-bird droppings. Compounding the disaster, rains accompanying El Niño flooded the normally arid coastal plains of Peru, drowning crops and eroding the coastline.

According to archeologist Michael Moseley of Chicago's Field Museum, similar El Niño rains may have brought about the collapse of the 12th Century Peruvian kingdom of the Chimu. After studying traces of a sophisticated irrigation system, apparently destroyed by floods around 1100 A.D., Moseley suggested that El Niño-induced rain wrecked the canals, rendering the farmland useless and leading to widespread famine. His theory is supported by a local legend that the kingdom suffered 30 days and nights of rain because the King had incurred the wrath of the gods. Seeing their farmland destroyed, the story goes, the people bound up the King and threw him in the ocean. The rains stopped, but famine and disease weakened the population, and the kingdom was conquered by an invading army.

To primitive people, angry gods would have been a far more plausible explanation for their misfortune than some incomprehensible connection between sea and sky. Indeed, only recently have scientists begun to understand the scale and complexity of the interaction that takes place over 72 per cent of the earth's surface. "It is beginning to dawn on us," noted a study published in 1969 by the National Academy of Sciences, "that on this global scale the atmosphere and the ocean are as closely linked as two coats of paint on a croquet ball."

In fact, the two entities are linked in so many ways that scientists have been frustrated repeatedly in their attempts to separate cause from effect.

It is clear, however, that ocean and atmosphere work in concert to moderate the earth's uneven absorption of solar heat. In essence, incoming solar

Normally, prevailing easterly trade winds
(*white arrows*) above and below the Equator
cause cold, nutrient-rich water (*blue*) to
well up from the ocean floor west of Peru. They
also hold the warm waters of the Equatorial
Countercurrent (*green*) at bay in mid-Pacific.

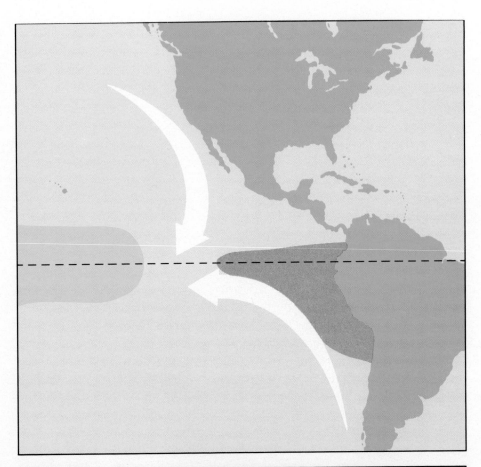

El Niño occurs when trade winds inexplicably
diminish and the warm countercurrent
smothers the coastal upwelling, with calamitous
effects on sea life and weather patterns.
In 1982 these effects were heightened by
extraordinary westerly winds (*red arrow*).

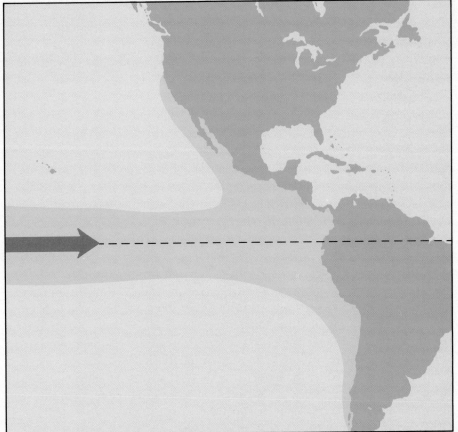

radiation, which passes through the atmosphere without appreciably affecting it, warms the ocean. The ocean in turn warms the air by reradiating heat into the atmosphere, which changes the heat into kinetic energy as wind. Winds and the currents they set in motion then act together to transport heat from its greatest concentration, near the Equator, to the cold higher latitudes.

While both the ocean and the atmosphere are set in motion by the sun, operate under the same laws of fluid dynamics and produce many of the same effects, there are of course fundamental differences in their behavior. The most significant of these differences arise from sea water's molecular density and weight; a section of ocean three feet deep weighs approximately as much as the entire column of air stretching above it to the edge of space. The denser a material is, the longer it takes to change temperature. A given amount of heat would take 3,000 times longer to raise the temperature of a body of water one degree than to warm the same volume of air at sea level.

Just as it warms more slowly than air, water is also slower to cool; it

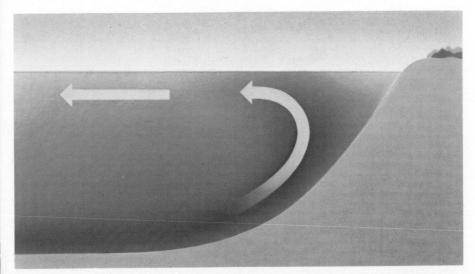

A wheeling, screaming flock of gulls feeds on ocean life nourished by the upwelling of nutrient-rich waters off the California coast. The diagram at right shows how winds blowing offshore or parallel to shore sweep aside surface waters, spurring a compensating upsurge of mineral-laden water from the deep.

stores heat, much as a battery absorbs electrical energy. So great, in fact, is the ocean's storage capacity that the upper 10 feet of the world's oceans holds as much heat as the entire atmosphere. Heat may be retained by the atmosphere for only a matter of days or, at most, weeks; the ocean, on the other hand, may not release its heat for years or, in the case of the deep ocean, even centuries. This long-term storage, transport and gradual release of heat benefits many countries where warmth from the sun is scant.

Atmosphere and ocean also work together to move heat from place to place through the hydrological cycle — the evaporation, condensation and precipitation of water. When ocean water evaporates, heat is removed from the water and, in effect, stored in the vapor. While this airborne moisture travels through the atmosphere, the heat remains latent — that is, it does not act to raise the temperature of its surroundings. But when the vapor condenses, into the water droplets that form clouds or into precipitation, the heat it took from the ocean is finally released to warm the air where condensation is taking place. Although the increments of heat involved are tiny, the total amounts are impressive. Most of the heat contained in the atmosphere derives from this release of latent heat. Each year the atmosphere absorbs an amount of ocean water that would lower the world's sea level by three feet if it were not replaced; but the moisture condenses and returns to the sea, 90 per cent of it directly, in the form of rain or snow, the rest falling first on land and running back to the sea in rivers.

On a global scale and over vast periods of time, the heat budget of the oceans balances; while every day heat is gained from the sun, lost to the air, and transferred from place to place by the hydrological cycle and the movement of currents, the average temperature of ocean water has remained stable for thousands of years. But during shorter periods and in certain regions of the ocean, the heat budget can register either a gain or a loss. Tropical oceans — which benefit from direct, year-round solar radiation, few clouds and clear waters easily penetrated by sunlight — collect and retain so much heat that they register an annual net gain. Middle latitudes absorb energy in the summer but release it in the winter, generally neither gaining nor losing heat in a year's time. Polar seas, where the sun never rises far above the horizon, suffer an annual heat loss.

Whenever two bodies of differing temperatures come in contact, heat

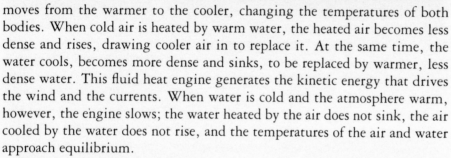

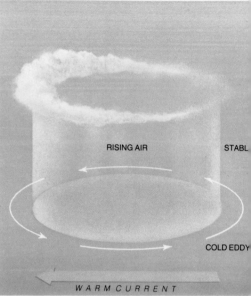

RISING AIR   STABL

COLD EDDY

WARM CURRENT

As seen from the Skylab spacecraft over the Caribbean, patches of clear air mark pools of cool water, 10 to 40 miles across, trapped within the warm, eddying flow of the Yucatan Current. The diagram above explains how the chill water cools the overlying air, stabilizing it and preventing cloud formation; at the eddy boundaries, the warm water of the current yields moist, buoyant air that rises to form clouds.

moves from the warmer to the cooler, changing the temperatures of both bodies. When cold air is heated by warm water, the heated air becomes less dense and rises, drawing cooler air in to replace it. At the same time, the water cools, becomes more dense and sinks, to be replaced by warmer, less dense water. This fluid heat engine generates the kinetic energy that drives the wind and the currents. When water is cold and the atmosphere warm, however, the engine slows; the water heated by the air does not sink, the air cooled by the water does not rise, and the temperatures of the air and water approach equilibrium.

The processes in the two fluids are inextricably linked: Air is set in motion by differences in temperature, and many such differences are induced by the ocean; the sea generates the wind that then moves the sea. The most immediate and visible evidence of this continuing interaction is the wave. But for all the deceptive simplicity of waves, they are generated by a complex interaction of physical forces that scientists do not fully understand.

One factor at work is the Bernoulli principle, which states that when a flow of air is constricted, as is the case when wind rides up over a wave, it speeds up, and as it does the pressure of the air drops. As the wind then dips into the hollow between two waves, it slows and its pressure increases. Because the water is pushed downward in the trough by the higher pressure and drawn upward at the crest by the reduced pressure, the wave height increases. A developing wave also receives an added push as the wind presses against its back; the air then rides over the top of the wave and swirls in a circle, blowing upward against the leading edge of the wave. These two forces work together to increase the height of the wave.

Energy is transferred to the water whenever the wind ruffles the sea surface, so the air momentarily slows down. When this air is overtaken by faster-moving air above it, the friction between the air layers that results from their differing velocities causes a vertical eddy, or turbulence, to form. The eddy lowers the air pressure just ahead of the wave crest and increases pressure behind the crest, thus tending to increase the wave's height.

Up to a point, the height of a wave is proportional to the speed of the wind. As a rule, the wave continues to rise until the wind speed reaches about 15 miles per hour. By then, the wave is so high that the crest outruns the body of the wave and topples, forming a turbulent whitecap. Sea water whips into more whitecaps than fresh water because the salt content produces more air bubbles and sustains them longer.

In recent years, scientists have discovered that the breaking of waves along a shore and the toppling of whitecaps on a wind-stirred sea play a crucial role in air-sea interaction and the hydrological cycle. A crashing wave, along with the action of both rain and snow striking the ocean surface, creates small air bubbles, which mix oxygen and other gases in the sea. Each tiny splash facilitates evaporation and lifts salt into the air. The salt molecules carried upward by wind become condensation nuclei — the tiny particles around which all precipitation forms — and as the infinitesimally small heart of each raindrop and snowflake, the salt returns to the sea.

Wave height, measured from crest to trough, is determined by three factors — the speed of the wind, the distance the wind has traveled across the water (known as fetch) and the wind's duration. Waves in bays and small gulfs never reach the size of those in the open sea despite high winds — gale-force winds with a fetch of 600 to 800 miles are necessary to generate a massive ocean wave.

Enormous waves at sea actually pose little threat to ships, since vessels pitch and roll with the undulating water. A greater threat is posed by huge breaking waves, which can topple hundreds of tons of water onto a vessel in a cascade capable of driving the ship to the bottom.

One of these monsters in the North Atlantic in 1966 smashed into the Italian passenger ship *Michelangelo* and broke windows 81 feet above her water line, flooding the bow section of the big liner and killing three passengers. Another breaking wave during a typhoon in the Pacific tore 90 feet off the bow of the heavy cruiser U.S.S. *Pittsburgh* in 1965. But the highest wave ever reliably recorded was measured by a watch officer aboard the naval tanker U.S.S. *Ramapo* in 1933.

In early February, en route from Manila to San Diego, the 478-foot *Ramapo* was thrashing along at the edge of a storm system that stretched all the way from Alaska to the mid-Pacific and eastward to lower California. This wide expanse of conflicting storms provided ideal conditions for winds with long fetches to generate huge waves.

On February 5, as the *Ramapo* crossed the 180th meridian — mid-Pacific — her barometer dropped to 29.58, and the winds from astern increased to gale force. She was entering a storm and would travel with it for four days. The next day the winds were gusting to 68 knots. In the early morning of February 7, Lieutenant (Jg.) Frederick C. Marggraff had the watch from midnight to 4 a.m. The sky had cleared somewhat, and the moon lit up a mountainous landscape of white-topped water.

Standing on the *Ramapo's* forward bridge and facing her stern as the full gale shrieked in the rigging, Marggraff watched each gigantic wave move toward the tanker, lift her stern skyward and rush on as the vessel settled in the trough. "The conditions for observing the seas from the ship were

Rating the Force of the Wind

The relationship between wind speed and wave height has always been of critical concern to mariners — especially the skippers of sailing vessels. In 1805 the British admiral Sir Francis Beaufort devised a scale for reckoning wind speed from the countenance of the sea.

Because it depends on an individual assessment of visual criteria, the Beaufort scale is not precise. Moreover, its numerical rankings of wind force, from 0, which represents a calm, to 12, for hurricane winds, do not represent equal increments of wind speed. And it can yield a reliable result only when the sea is fully developed — when the wind has held steady long enough to produce waves that reflect its full strength. But for the sailors of the past, who lacked the instruments to measure wind speed directly, Beaufort's guide was vital in deciding when to add or furl sail.

BEAUFORT NUMBER 1 — LIGHT AIR
Small ripples give the sea a scaly appearance, indicating a wind speed of from one to three miles per hour.

BEAUFORT NUMBER 6 — STRONG BREEZE
Medium-sized waves, numerous whitecaps, and blowing spray characterize a wind of 25 to 31 miles per hour.

BEAUFORT NUMBER 8 — GALE
High, breaking waves and streaks of foam across the surface of the sea indicate a wind of 39 to 46 miles per hour.

BEAUFORT NUMBER 2 — LIGHT BREEZE
A smooth sea patterned with tiny wavelets denotes a wind speed of from four to seven miles per hour.

BEAUFORT NUMBER 4 — MODERATE BREEZE
A sea dappled with small waves that occasionally crest to form whitecaps is produced by a wind of 13 to 18 miles per hour.

BEAUFORT NUMBER 9 — STRONG GALE
Very high waves release sheets of spray that reduce visibility; the wind has reached 47 to 54 miles per hour.

BEAUFORT NUMBER 11 — VIOLENT STORM
Waves high enough to hide small ships, frothy wave crests and limited visibility indicate a wind of 64 to 72 miles per hour.

ideal," the captain's official report later recorded. "We were running directly downwind and with the sea. There were no cross seas and therefore no peaks along wave crests. There was practically no rolling and the pitching motion was easy because of the fact that the sides of the waves were materially longer than the ship."

Looking aft, Marggraff could see high over his head on the mainmast 150 feet astern an iron strap on the boom near the crow's nest. Like the other watch officer, he used this as a fix in trying to gauge the height of the waves rolling down on the tanker. As the *Ramapo's* stern settled into a trough, Marggraff sighted across the boom strap at the top of a truly phenomenal wave that hid the horizon. He immediately calculated a simple trigonometric equation: He knew the heights of the boom strap and the bridge (plus Marggraff's eye-level height of 5 feet 11 inches) and the length of the tanker from stern to bridge; thus he could work out the one unknown line of the triangle, the height from the trough to the line from bridge to wave crest. An earlier wave had measured 82 feet, another 107. According to Marggraff's calculations, the Everest of them all soared 112 feet high.

The *Ramapo's* wave watchers, as their report points out, were able to make an accurate measurement of their record breaker because there were no cross seas — a perilous situation occurring when opposing waves, driven by high winds, meet head on and send each other cresting even higher. One area notorious for such turbulent meetings of wave systems is off the Cape of Good Hope, where the waters of the South Atlantic and Indian Oceans meet. In 1964, for example, the steamship *Edinburgh Castle* was breasting a heavy southwest swell off the Cape when she was struck by an unexpected wave that roared over her in a 20-foot wall of water. She barely managed to climb back to the surface in time for the next wave.

The big waves stirred up by a storm at sea will last long after the storm has subsided. In great moving swells the waves can roll across an entire ocean to come crashing ashore on a far continent or island. In October 1958, towering 30-foot waves suddenly roared out of a calm sea to batter the tropical island of Barbados in the West Indies. The monstrous crests tossed fishing boats onto the beaches and flooded coastal homes. Caught totally by surprise, weather forecasters hastily reexamined their charts and pinpointed the culprit as a North Atlantic cyclone that two days earlier had whipped up the sea east of Newfoundland, more than 2,000 miles away.

Yet despite the impressive size and speed of a racing wave, the water itself scarcely moves at all. If it did, mountains of water would plow across the sea, followed by vast floods pouring into the gaps left behind. It was the German scientist Franz Gerstner who realized, in the early 1800s, that the water in a wave actually moves in a circular orbit, as the motion of a drift bottle bobbing on the surface demonstrates. Instead of rushing along with the wave, the bottle rises over the wave as it passes. As the wave's peak rushes on, the bottle dips, sliding down the back of the wave. Sinking into the trough, the bottle rises again with the next wave, moving forward almost imperceptibly.

While inconsequential in an individual wave, this forward motion, backed by a prevailing wind traveling over thousands of miles, accumulates into the powerful global force of the ocean current. But surface currents, which stir the oceans to a depth of about 300 feet, are but the lower boundary of an intricate interlacing of ocean and atmosphere. Just as prevailing winds tend to draw cold polar air toward the Equator and warm tropical air toward the Poles, the ocean currents circulate stored heat in much the same patterns. And although the faster-moving and faster-changing atmosphere transports two thirds of the heat that moves from the tropics to the midlatitudes, the ocean—because it stores greater quantities of heat—provides the slow, steady warming influence that yields long-term climatic effect.

The dramatic effect of warm-water currents is best observed in the mild weather of the British Isles. Although they are on the same latitude as frigid Labrador, their average temperature is much higher in the winter, largely because of tropical waters that have retained their heat for thousands of miles. The sun-warmed currents of the westward-running North and South Equatorial Currents, bouncing off North America, are deflected by the Coriolis effect northward and back across the North Atlantic in the Gulf Stream; the stream is so rapid and water's heat content so great that when the North Atlantic Drift branches off from the swirling eddies of the Gulf Stream to race past the British Isles, it still warms the atmosphere enough to nurture palm trees that have been transplanted to Ullapool, Scotland.

The Gulf Stream's northeast-flowing offshoot not only keeps its warmth, it also evidences another characteristic of sea water, especially during the winter. As the surface water releases heat and cools, its density increases; it sinks and is replaced by the layers of warmer water beneath, preserving the current's beneficent effect even longer.

As a result of this influence, England generally has a far milder winter than American locations of much lower latitude. And Reykjavik, the capital of Iceland, has warmer winters than New York City, which is 2,400 miles farther south. Norwegian ports are usually free of ice when those in the Baltic, hundreds of miles south but outside the influence of the North Atlantic Drift, are frozen. And at the other end of the earth, Antarctica would be colder still were it not for currents bringing warm waters into the circumpolar West Wind Drift in the Southern Ocean to moderate the climate of the continent.

The full range of climatological effects is also played out in the North Pacific, where the Kuroshio Current brings warm water up from the North Equatorial Current, modifying southern Japan's climate. Then, north of Japan, the Kuroshio meets the cold waters of the Oyashio Current coming down from the Okhotsk and Bering Seas. Northern Japan, as a result, has more than its share of fogs and storms, caused by the clashing temperatures of both currents. The interchange of water and atmosphere continues as the Kuroshio Current becomes the North Pacific Current when it turns eastward across the Pacific. The Aleutians are bathed in fog as the last warmth of the current is dispersed by frigid waters from the Bering Sea. By the time the North Pacific Current turns south along the North American continent and becomes the California Current, its waters are so chilly that the Washington, Oregon and California coasts are cooler than normal for their latitude in the summer. San Francisco does not attain its warmest temperatures until September, when the sun has had all spring and summer to warm the stubbornly cold California Current; 100 miles inland at Sacramento, where the ocean has less influence, July is the hot month.

Ocean currents may in fact even be responsible for deserts. Where cool currents run along a coast, their water chills the overlying air, causing it to sink. Little evaporation takes place, no latent heat is released and conse-

A towering wave dumps hundreds of tons of sea water onto the bow of a supertanker rounding the Cape of Good Hope. When waves generated by Antarctic storms collide with the powerful Agulhas Current, which flows southward along the East African coast, they grow abruptly steeper and taller, commonly reaching heights of 70 feet.

quently little rain falls. Thus the cold Canaries Current helps account for the aridity of the Sahara, as the Benguela Current along the southwestern coast of Africa does for the Namib Desert and the Peru Current does for the coastal deserts of Peru and northern Chile.

Ocean temperatures may be responsible for the rainiest places in the world. An average of 460 inches of rain falls annually on the soaring cliffs of Mount Waialeale on Hawaii's Kauai Island. Onshore winds, saturated with evaporation after crossing the Pacific Ocean, unleash the downpour. For similar reasons the Bahia Felix coast of Chile, near the southern tip of South America, experiences rainfall on the average of 325 days a year.

Ocean-surface temperatures can do far more than generate rain. For example, high surface temperatures favor the formation of waterspouts, first cousins to the tornado. Because of their ephemeral nature, waterspouts are not well understood. So-called fair-weather waterspouts develop at sea level and climb toward overhanging clouds, while tornadic waterspouts, which pack enough of a destructive wallop to threaten a boat, generally drop out of the leading edge of advancing cold fronts, much like their fearsome land-bound counterparts. During their brief lives, rarely more than 60 minutes, waterspouts can be buffeted by prevailing winds into fantastic contortions and have been known to reach nearly a mile into the air. While they are spectacular, waterspouts nonetheless rarely inflict serious damage.

Warm ocean waters, in the right swirling patterns, can be responsible for the most destructive of all storms — the tropical cyclone. Heat and moisture released into the atmosphere from warm tropical water fuels this whirling heat engine (sent spinning by the Coriolis effect), which frequently goes marching across the ocean to smash ashore with furious winds and drowning rain. Called a hurricane in the Americas and a typhoon or tropical cyclone in the East, these storms can form only over the warm equatorial currents of the North Atlantic, Pacific and Indian Oceans. If the storm moves over cooler water before reaching land, its heat engine slows, the cyclonic circulation disperses and the storm dies.

Sometimes the tables are turned and local weather conditions exert a profound influence on the ocean. The North Indian Ocean, for example, is unique in that its currents respond directly to annual changes in wind patterns. The currents of the South Indian Ocean rotate in the counterclockwise gyre typical of the Southern Hemisphere, which is relatively unaffected by the seasonal change in the area's powerful prevailing winds — the monsoons. But north of the Equator the Indian Ocean's currents change course twice a year in response to the monsoon winds.

Across nearly half of the globe, from Africa through the Middle East, most of Asia and Australia, the summer sun heats up the continental land masses, especially the wide desert areas, and lowers the pressure of the corresponding air masses. But the moist air over the Indian Ocean maintains a higher pressure because the temperature of the ocean surface does not increase as quickly as that of land. During the monsoon season, from May to October, air circulates around the high-pressure region and flows into the low-pressure trough as strong southwesterly winds over the western Indian Ocean. These winds, coupled with the Coriolis effect, push the northern Indian Ocean's currents into a clockwise gyre. But during the winter months, from November through April, the sun moves southward, the land masses of the Northern Hemisphere cool faster than the ocean waters, and

The ocean and the atmosphere work together as a kind of heat engine that converts the energy of sunlight into a moving global mosaic of prevailing winds and corresponding surface currents.

Most solar energy striking the earth passes through the atmosphere and is absorbed by the planet's surface — 72 per cent of which is covered by water. The sun-warmed ocean then heats the lower atmosphere. Fully half of the energy transfer takes place as heated water turns into vapor, rises from the ocean and condenses into clouds and precipitation, only then releasing the heat it absorbed from the ocean as it evaporated.

Solar radiation is most intense at the Equator, where the surface waters are heated fiercely all year long. The rising of this warm, buoyant air draws in air from north and south; this air movement, deflected westward by the earth's rotation, comprises the area's prevailing winds. Spreading poleward at high altitude, the warm air cools and sinks, contributing to temperate-latitude prevailing winds or circulating back toward the Equator and completing the cycle of air movement.

The atmospheric circulation in turn sets the sea surface in motion, driving current gyres that thrust cold water toward the Equator and channel the warm tropical water into temperate latitudes.

A schematic diagram shows how ocean and atmosphere interact to convert radiant energy from the sun into kinetic energy, or motion. Solar energy absorbed by the ocean heats the air, spurring the atmospheric circulation that powers the currents of the water's surface.

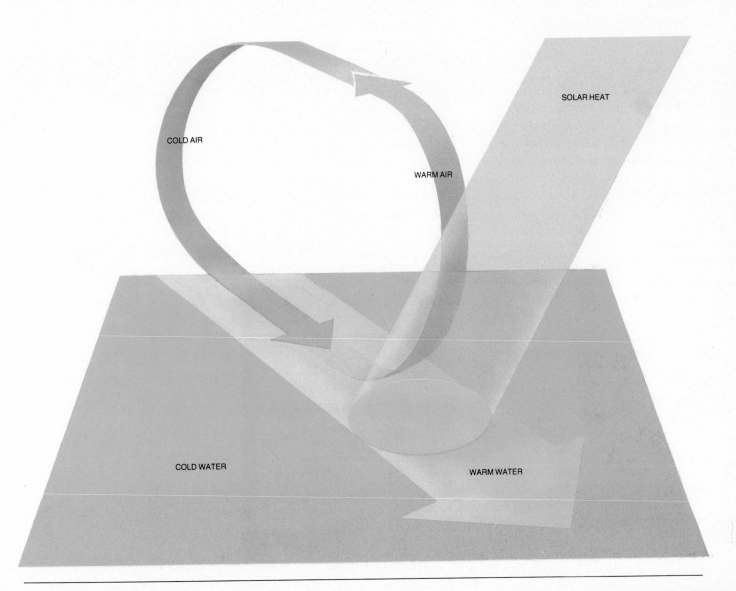

COLD AIR

SOLAR HEAT

WARM AIR

COLD WATER

WARM WATER

the atmospheric pressure differential between ocean and continent reverses. Now the winds blow from the northeast, and they set up a current in the North Indian Ocean that turns counterclockwise, in the opposite direction from the other large Northern Hemisphere gyres.

During the 1920s, while British meteorologist Sir Gilbert Walker was stationed in India, he sought a method of forecasting the monsoon rainfall that accompanies the seasonal change in wind direction and is critical to the country's agriculture. He did not find it, but he stumbled on something else, a remarkable pattern of low-latitude atmospheric circulation that he called the Southern Oscillation. Many years later, his observation would provide the framework for solving the riddle of El Niño. As Walker described his discovery, "When pressure is high (relative to the mean) in the Pacific Ocean it tends to be low in the Indian Ocean from Africa to Australia; these conditions are associated with low temperatures in both of these areas, and rainfall varies in the opposite direction to pressure."

Walker found that every few years, pressures rise in the low-pressure region centered over Indonesia and fall in the region of high pressure over the southeastern Pacific. But he could find no cause and no explanation for what sustained the atmospheric seesaw.

In 1931, German oceanographer Gerhard Schott noted that local fluctuations in atmospheric pressure off the coast of South America coincided with the appearance of El Niño. But nearly 30 years passed before the next step was taken toward an understanding of how El Niño and the ocean-wide pressure shifts of the Southern Oscillation were related.

The man who achieved the breakthrough bore one of the great names in the physical sciences. Jacob Bjerknes was a scion of the famed Norwegian family that founded modern meteorology. His grandfather, mathematician Carl Bjerknes, had made advances in fluid-dynamics theories, which his father, Vilhelm, applied to atmospheric and oceanic circulation. At the small Bergen Geophysical Institute, Vilhelm Bjerknes assembled a scientific team (including his son Jacob) that developed exciting new meteorology theories. The team introduced the concept of fronts between air masses and pioneered the modern understanding of cyclones — stormy areas of low-pressure wind circulation — that develop on and travel along the fronts.

In 1939 Jacob Bjerknes was on an American lecture tour with his family, and the outbreak of World War II in Europe prevented his return home. Bjerknes became chairman of the new Department of Meteorology at the University of California at Los Angeles. There he studied the effect on the atmosphere of fluctuations in ocean-surface temperature in the tropics. He used the word "teleconnections" to describe the atmospheric links between the tropics and higher latitudes. These connections included the Southern Oscillation and more; he traced climatic change in Russia to temperature changes in the Pacific Ocean and in 1961 published a paper on El Niño.

Bjerknes' studies indicated that enormous changes in atmospheric circulation patterns — the Southern Oscillation — over the equatorial Pacific were linked to the diminished trade winds that preceded the onset of El Niño. Under normal circumstances, the trade winds off the Peruvian coast move water to the west, drawing cooler deep water up to the ocean surface. Bjerknes reasoned that a slackening of the trade winds would cause the warm water that had collected in the western parts of the Pacific to flow

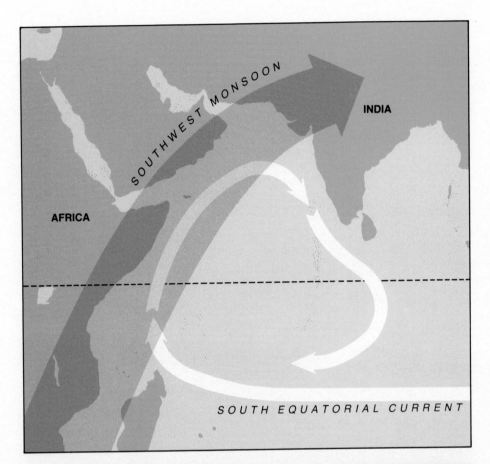

The circulation of the Indian Ocean during the summer months, diagramed at right, is powered by a prevailing wind called the Southwest Monsoon, which blows toward a region of low pressure over Asia created by air rising from the sun-heated ground. The resulting clockwise current gyre swirls up the coast of Africa and eastward toward India.

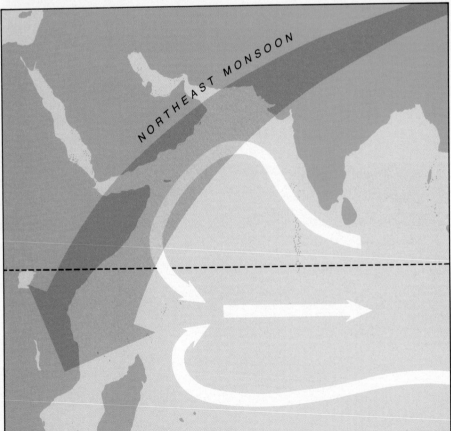

As the Asian land mass cools in winter, a high-pressure zone of sinking air replaces the low and propels winds that rush seaward as the Northeast Monsoon. The wind-driven ocean currents do an about-face, coursing now from India toward Africa.

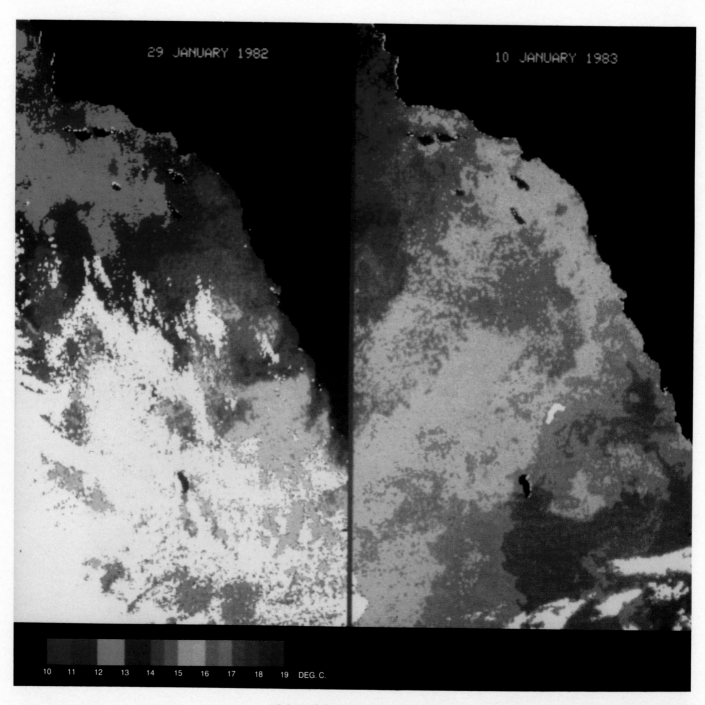

29 JANUARY 1982   10 JANUARY 1983

10 11 12 13 14 15 16 17 18 19 DEG. C.

Color-coded satellite images of sea-surface temperatures in January 1982 (recorded along the stretch of California coast outlined at right), portray the coastal waters' normal chill in greens and blues *(above, left)*. A year later, at the height of the 1982-1983 El Niño phenomenon *(above, right)*, a scarlet tongue of warm water protrudes into the area.

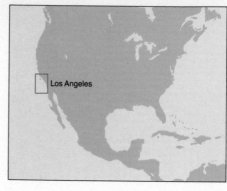

Los Angeles

back across the ocean and thus suppress the cool upwelling along the coast.

Influenced by Bjerknes' work, Klaus Wyrtki of the University of Hawaii collected temperature and sea-level measurements from 33 Pacific island and coastal sites to offer still stronger evidence that El Niño was an ocean-wide sea-air interaction. He proposed that the strength of the trade winds occasionally intensifies for a year or more, drawn westward by an unusually strong low-pressure area over Indonesia, and drags surface water to the west. Data showed sea-level build-up before the 1972 El Niño of as much as a foot and a half along the coasts of Southeast Asia and a simultaneous drop in sea level along South American shores, much as water can be blown against the side of a cup. When atmospheric pressure again oscillates and the Indonesian low weakens, Wyrtki held, the water beneath it flows back across the Pacific in an internal movement known as a Kelvin wave. Rolling eastward along the Equator at a few yards a second, the subsurface bulge of warm water amplifies the existing Equatorial Countercurrent and raises sea level as it moves across the ocean, reaching South America several weeks later. It is this thick layer of warm water, Wyrtki said, that suppresses the Peruvian upwelling.

The work of Bjerknes and Wyrtki heightened scientific interest in El Niño, as did the 1972 episode, and spawned many data-collecting studies using weather satellites, drift buoys, and research and merchant ships.

Yet as sophisticated as knowledge of El Niño had become in a decade, no one saw the phenomenon coming in 1982. Eugene Rasmusson, chief of the Climate Analysis Center diagnostic branch at the U.S. Weather Service, said later, "Even in September, when it was staring us in the eye, a few people were still saying, 'This can't be happening.'" It came at the wrong time, six months later than the normal onset of the El Niño current. It happened in the wrong place, with sea-surface temperature changes first noted in the mid-Pacific, not off the South American coast. Trade winds in the western Pacific had not been unusually strong the year before. "We've learned," said a rueful Rasmusson, "that we have to unlearn some things."

Still, he pointed out, progress was made. "Some of the teleconnections that we'd had only weak or inconclusive evidence of turned out to be very strong, such as a strengthening of the jet stream, and wet weather across the U.S. Perhaps this El Niño differed from the norm more than most. Maybe now we'll be able to get down to the core of what's really necessary for El Niño, then we'll be able to understand how the differences came about."

With data-collecting systems in place, scientists were able to obtain more information about El Niño than ever before. Temperature readings showed an unprecedented northward extension of warm water. After reaching the South American coast, the heated tropical water spread as far as Alaska, disrupting fish populations as it traveled. Squid normally harvested off California disappeared, apparently moving to deeper, cooler waters to the west. A four-degree temperature rise in northern California waters dispersed the salmon, whose place was taken by shrimp, barracuda and bonito.

The combination of air heated and moistened by this intrusion of warm water and the cold water and air common to the higher latitudes increased the strength of the jet stream, the ribbon of fast-moving air that normally arcs west to east high above the North Pacific and the mid-United States. The stream speeded up and veered 600 miles to the south across Mexico and the Gulf Coast. Because of it, surprised airplane pilots found their flight

times from Hawaii to California cut by as much as an hour. The off-course jet stream trapped a dry high-pressure zone over Mexico and permitted storm-bearing low-pressure air to invade California, unleashing torrential rain and spawning enormous ocean swells along the coast. As it raced up the East Coast, the stream channeled a seemingly endless series of rainstorms and snowstorms to the southern Atlantic states.

Oscillations in atmospheric pressure clearly altered the transport of heat and moisture over all the land masses bordering the Pacific. Disruption from a lesser Atlantic oscillation was blamed for the drought in West Africa. The same large region of high-pressure air that invaded Indonesia apparently brought the drought to southern Africa and India.

With the world's weather turned upside down, research meteorologist Jerome Namias of the Scripps Institution of Oceanography in La Jolla, California, grappled with El Niño's crazy twists in drafting long-range weather forecasts. Trained as a meteorologist, Namias had found in the 1950s that long-term weather patterns have a dramatic effect on sea-surface temperature, or SST, creating anomalies that in turn affect weather patterns. Struck by the impact each had on the other, Namias assembled thousands of ocean-temperature readings taken monthly by ships, planes, buoys and remote-sensing satellites assisting the program. Using this information, he developed methods of estimating future trends in atmospheric pressure and wind patterns. His annual forecasts, issued every fall and predicting the weather for the coming winter throughout the United States, soon won him a reputation for remarkable accuracy for such long-range assessments.

His research prompted Namias to delve still deeper into the origins of El Niño, beyond even the Southern Oscillation. He developed a theory that the initial weakening of the trade winds that marked the onset of El Niño could be traced back to SST anomalies — pools of water as much as five degrees warmer or cooler than surrounding seas in the subtropics and higher latitudes. Such anomalies, frequently as large as a fourth of the area of the North Pacific and often signaling disturbances in the deep ocean, exert atmospheric influence measurable for weeks, months or even years. Possibly, buried among those anomalies, lies the particular sequence of events destined to trigger El Niño.

With their success in treating the ocean and the atmosphere as inextricably linked fluids that continuously reflect each other's complex motions, scientists such as Namias and his colleagues have uncovered some of the myriad complexities facing those who would understand either entity in detail. And yet their discoveries hint, ever more strongly, at an underlying unity of principles and forces that, when grasped, may permit scientists to read in the slow changes of the sea what lies ahead for the more volatile realms of the sky. Ω

Born of a subtle interplay of air and ocean, wisps of Arctic "sea smoke" veil the surface of the Bering Sea. Sea smoke forms when chill, dry air flows from a cold land mass or an expanse of pack ice over warmer open water, causing water vapor rising from the sea to condense.

THE QUEST FOR NEPTUNE'S POWER

The world's oceans are charged with energy that could one day ease the world's dependence on dwindling supplies of oil, coal and gas. The energy comes from the sun; first it is stored as heat, then much of it activates the global wind machine *(page 89)* that is responsible for waves and currents. A smaller proportion of the sun's energy is absorbed by the green plants of the sea and stored as carbohydrates.

Theoretically, the waves striking a 60-mile stretch of coast contain enough energy to supply power for a million homes. And there is enough heat in the surface waters of the Gulf of Mexico to produce 30 per cent of the electricity that is used in the U.S. Gulf States.

The problem for scientists is how to tap these endlessly renewable resources. The energy is dispersed throughout enormous volumes of water, and the cost of equipment large enough to winnow significant quantities of usable energy from the water remains prohibitive. For example, one ocean-energy project would produce methane—a substitute for natural gas—from giant kelp, the species of fast-growing seaweed shown below, by harvesting the plant and decomposing it in airtight tanks. But a kelp plantation capable of meeting U.S. requirements for gas would occupy tens of thousands of square miles.

Sunlight streams through fronds of giant kelp, a seaweed that grows as much as two feet a day and attains lengths of 200 feet. A hundred pounds of kelp, when decomposed, yields a pound — six cubic feet — of methane gas.

A harvesting boat off the California coast cuts and loads giant kelp for use in the manufacture of industrial chemicals. Kelp could be a major source of methane gas, but at a cost that is not competitive with petroleum products.

A Duck That
Bobs for Kilowatts

As they move in unending progression across thousands of miles of ocean, waves carry with them enough energy to satisfy the entire world's demand for electric power. A variety of schemes, all involving the ingenious application of simple mechanical principles, have been proposed to capture some fraction of that energy before it is spent as surf.

One of the most promising plans involves the deployment of a hollow float of reinforced concrete, 100 feet long and 60 feet across, known as Salter's Duck.

Named for its designer, Stephen Salter of Scotland's University of Edinburgh, and for its resemblance to the profile of a duck's body, the ponderous device would be mounted on a shaft with its tapered end pointing seaward. With each incoming wave, the float would tilt upward, absorbing the waveborne energy so completely as to leave calm water in its lee. Inside the shaft, pumps activated by the rocking motion would circulate oil through a turbine, which in turn would drive an electric generator.

Salter envisions mooring a line of 20 Ducks, linked by a jointed shaft that would flex in heavy seas, along a wave-lashed shore such as the coast of the Outer Hebrides Islands, west of Scotland. Power from each Duck would flow into a cable running along the shaft and across the seabed to shore. A $1/10$-scale prototype of such a wave-power facility has been tested in the stormy waters of Loch Ness, and Salter believes that a full-sized array could power a city of 85,000.

In an artist's conception, a line of Salter's Ducks rides the waves, absorbing each undulation (*inset*) and converting its energy to electric current. To reduce stresses on the shaft, which could measure a half mile in length, the unit is moored at an angle to the waves, allowing the Ducks to absorb each wave progressively.

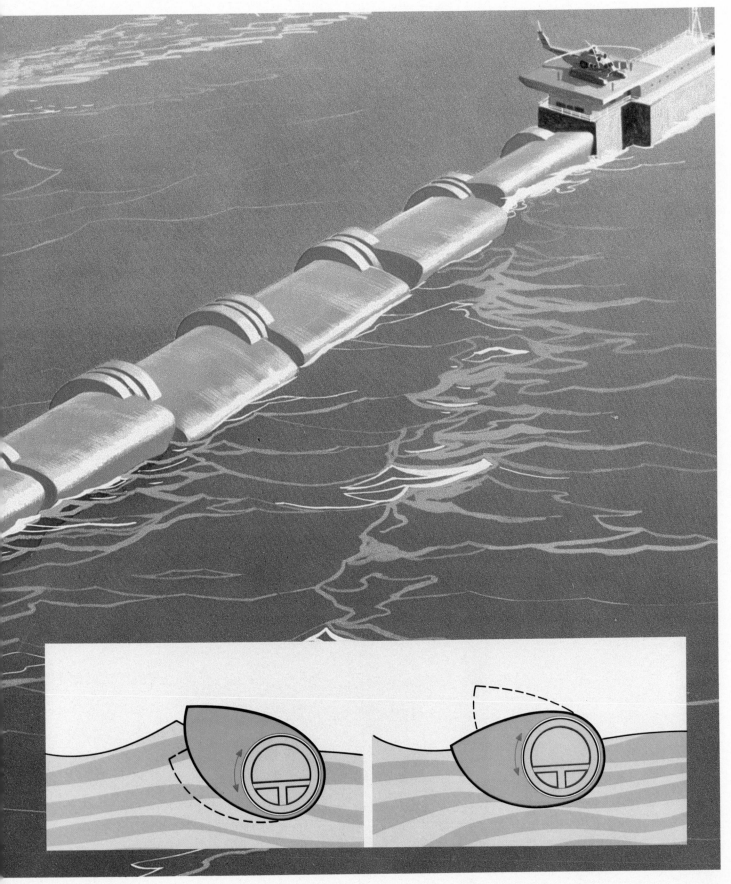

Bags of Air to Trap the Waves

Another British device for extracting energy from waves, as grand in scale as Salter's Duck and as simple in principle, is the SEA Clam, designed by a firm called Sea Energy Associates and a team of engineers at Lanchester Polytechnic in Coventry, England.

The Clam consists of a floating concrete tube, sealed at the ends and faced with air bladders of fabric and rubber; its name came from an earlier design, in which the bladders were protected by clamlike movable steel plates. Moored offshore, the Clam would be placed so the bags faced incoming waves.

As each wave crashed into the Clam, air would be driven out of the bladders through ducts connecting them with the concrete spine; when the pressure of the wave died away, air compressed within the tube would rush back into the bags, reinflating them by the time the next wave arrived. As air coursed back and forth through the ducts, turbines mounted in the passages would spin, driving generators that would send current to shore through a submarine cable.

The Clam, like other wave-energy devices, does not promise soon to become a major source of power: Present designs could not offer electricity at prices competitive with conventional power stations. But wave-power facilities might prove economical for isolated coastal settlements that now rely on costly diesel generators for electric power.

SEA Clam wave-power stations, tethered to moored floats that act as shock absorbers in heavy seas, are pummeled by waves in this artist's conception. A prototype Clam, tested in Loch Ness, measured 90 feet in length, but a full-sized device would stretch 900 feet, with air bladders 80 feet wide.

100

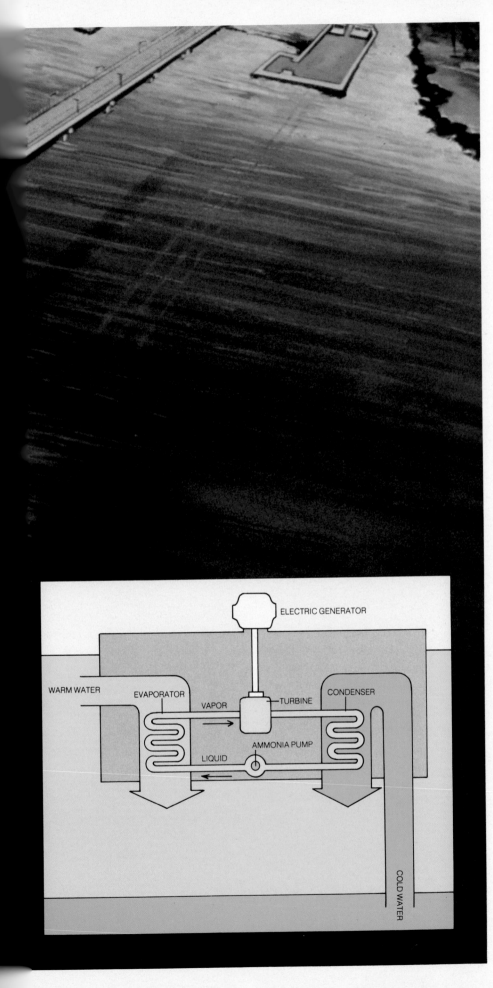

Plumbing the Depths for Electricity

By exploiting temperature differences between the surface and the depths, a process called Ocean Thermal Energy Conversion (OTEC) would tap the solar energy stored as heat in ocean waters.

The warmest water (as high as 85° F. in the tropics) is found in a surface layer a few hundred feet thick at most. Several thousand feet below, water temperature falls to about 40° F. In the most common OTEC design, a volatile liquid such as ammonia would be circulated through pipes warmed by surface water; the ammonia would boil and yield a stream of pressurized vapor that would spin a turbine and generate electric power. The spent vapor would then pass through a condenser immersed in cold water pumped from the ocean depths and emerge as a liquid, ready to cycle through the system again.

OTEC can operate only where surface waters are at least 40° warmer than deep layers, and certain proposals envision floating plants that could roam tropical oceans, searching for optimum temperature conditions. The power would then be transmitted to shore by submarine cables or supplied to seagoing factories requiring large amounts of electricity.

Even the warmest sea water yields comparatively little energy per unit of volume; to match the output of a large 1,000-megawatt conventional generating station, an OTEC plant would have to circulate 10 million tons of sea water per hour — a rate of flow greater than that of the Nile. The water pumps required would dwarf any now in existence, and the plant's cold-water inlet pipe would represent an unparalleled feat of engineering — it would have to be more than 130 feet in diameter and extend to a depth of at least 2,500 feet.

An artist's rendition of plans for a commercial OTEC plant at Kahe Point, Oahu, suggests the enormity of a land-based plant; this one would produce 40 megawatts of electricity — 1/10 the output of a typical coal-fired plant. The schematic diagram (*inset*) shows how ammonia would be boiled by surface water, then condensed again by cold water pumped from the depths two and a half miles offshore.

ELECTRIC GENERATOR

WARM WATER   EVAPORATOR   VAPOR   TURBINE   CONDENSER

LIQUID   AMMONIA PUMP

COLD WATER

Chapter 4

HIDDEN STIRRINGS IN THE DEEP

The British slave trader *Earl of Halifax* was in most respects an ordinary participant in the long and sordid history of slavery. But on a 1751 voyage from England to West Africa, a measurement was taken from the vessel's deck that made history of a more elevated kind; it was the beginning of a long series of investigations that would reveal, slowly at first but at an accelerating pace, the details of an enormous, hidden pattern of deep-sea water movements. Masses of near-freezing water — as much as is found in the surface currents — would be discovered to be oozing along the sea floors from the Poles to the Equator and back, from ocean to ocean, and ultimately all the way around the world. These sluggish migrations take place mostly at depths greater than 10,000 feet — too deep to have been noted by mariners in the normal course of events and, until recently, too remote to have been plumbed at all except in clumsy, isolated measurements.

The first such measurement was obtained off the West African coast when Captain Henry Ellis, the master of the *Earl of Halifax,* lowered over the gunwale a "bucket sea gauge" — little more than a covered wooden pail fitted with a thermometer. Water skimmed from the sea surface registered 84° F. — a temperature consistent with the torrid weather through which the ship was sailing. But when Ellis lowered the bucket to a depth of a mile, the water he retrieved was no warmer than 53° F. He assumed, correctly, that the sample had warmed by several degrees during the time it took to haul it from the depths, and that the actual temperature of the deep water was lower still. For Ellis, the chill water had practical rather than scientific value, as he later reported: "This experiment, which seem'd at first mere food for curiosity, became in the interim very useful to us. By its means we supplied our cold bath, and cooled our wines or water at pleasure, which is vastly agreeable in this burning climate."

But more scientific minds eventually grasped a greater significance in Ellis' discovery. Chill water deep in a lake in the temperate latitudes is a relic of winter cold, but Ellis had made his measurement in a region of constant summer. The great British scientist and statesman Benjamin Thompson, Count Rumford, guessed that the water that chilled Ellis' wine must have flowed into the tropics from cooler regions. "It appears to me," he wrote in 1797, "to be extremely difficult, if not quite impossible, to account for this degree of cold at the bottom of the sea in the torrid zone, on any other supposition than that of cold current from the poles."

In spite of Count Rumford's insightful suggestion that something was in motion in the depths, the subject was not pursued for more than a century

Just beneath the surface of the Mediterranean, a diver photographs the track of a sinking dye pellet, looped and knotted by the motions of distinct but invisible water layers. In the depths of the world's oceans, water layers thousands of feet thick circulate independently.

after Ellis' pioneering measurement. One reason for this was the lack of any way to get accurate temperature readings from the deep waters: Crushing water pressures compressed the thermometer bulbs of the day, squeezing mercury up into the stem and yielding an erroneous reading. But by 1872, when the British research ship *Challenger* began its four-year reconnaissance of the world's oceans, thermometers had been devised with protective bulbs that resisted the pressures of the depths and recorded accurately both the maximum and the minimum temperatures of the water layers through which they were lowered.

As a result, the *Challenger* scientists amassed large numbers of deep-ocean temperature profiles. The picture that emerged as scientists sifted through the data during the decades following the expedition was described by Alexander Buchan in an 1895 appendix to the *Challenger Report*. He noted that the coldest deepwater temperatures were found in the Southern Hemisphere and that the readings became progressively warmer at increased distances from Antarctica. According to his analysis, the coldest ocean basins are those that have direct links to the seas around Antarctica, and he identified these southern seas as the source of the frigid bottom water found throughout the world's oceans: "There can be no doubt that these very low deep-sea temperatures have their origin in the Southern or Antarctic Ocean, the icy cold waters of which are propagated northward, the rate of propagation being so slight as to be regarded as a slow creep rather than as a distinctly recognizable movement of the water." But this simple picture grew ever more complicated as deep-ocean research advanced.

The voyage of the German steamer *Meteor,* which set out from the North German port of Wilhelmshaven on April 16, 1925, was the first oceanographic expedition devoted primarily to the study of circulation. The ship — actually a converted gunboat, on loan from the German Navy — was lavishly outfitted with thermometers and sample bottles, echo sounders for charting bottom contours that influence the flow of deep water, and a shipboard laboratory for the chemical analysis of sea water. And the scientists aboard the *Meteor* were well prepared for their task in another sense: They were well versed in techniques of oceanographic research developed in the 1890s by Scandinavian scientists — in particular, the Swedish chemists Gustav Ekman and Otto Pettersson — in the course of detailed surveys of the Baltic and North Seas. By analyzing measurements of water temperature and salinity taken at numerous carefully chosen sounding stations, oceanographers could map the probable distribution of water properties throughout enormous volumes of ocean, and infer the extent and direction of distinct, moving masses of water.

But the financially strapped German government could not afford to equip the *Meteor* with expensive diesel engines, and even with every spare cranny in its narrow hull packed with stores of coal, the *Meteor* could not spend long periods at sea. Plans for a global survey of the oceans had to be dropped in favor of an exploration of the narrower expanse of the Atlantic. But what the *Meteor* expedition lacked in geographic scope, it made up in thoroughness: In the course of two years, it traversed the Atlantic 13 times at different latitudes, collecting 9,000 readings of temperature and salinity and making 33,000 echo soundings that revealed the contours of the ocean floor. And the 16 volumes of data published after the expedition returned to port presented the most comprehensive portrait to date of deep circulation.

Although restricted to a single ocean, the *Meteor* observations have proved so reliable that present-day oceanographers still draw on them.

The data from the *Meteor* showed that a layer of so-called Antarctic Bottom Water, easily recognized by its characteristic combination of low temperature and high salinity, can be found at depths below 14,000 feet as far from its source in the Antarctic seas as the latitude of the Caribbean. In the North Atlantic, the *Meteor* traced a slightly shallower mass of water, located between 5,000 and 13,000 feet down, that was even saltier than the Antarctic Bottom Water, but not quite so cold. This water mass — called North Atlantic Deep Water — spreads southward from the latitude of Greenland all the way to Argentina. The *Meteor* data also revealed a second layer of Antarctic water, centered at a depth of about 3,000 feet and moving northward over the North Atlantic water. As cold as the North Atlantic Deep Water but lower in salinity than either of the underlying layers, this water was dubbed, in the *Meteor* reports, the Antarctic Intermediate Water.

Although the *Meteor* measurements delineated the general arrangement and directions of the deepwater masses in the Atlantic, "the question of the actual character of the circulation processes cannot be answered," as expedition member Georg Wüst wrote in 1928. "What we can see in the thermal and saline structure is actually the end effect of these deepwater movements on the layering; the movements in detail remain puzzling." For want of evidence to the contrary, most oceanographers tended to accept the simplest explanation that fitted the observed distribution of water: a picture of slow, creeping water motions taking place across the entire width of the ocean, nowhere concentrated in a flow strong enough that it could be described as a current.

During the decades that followed the *Meteor* expedition, Wüst and other oceanographers attempted to construct mathematical models of the movements in the depths by analyzing the deepwater findings of the voyage with a set of equations known as the dynamical method. According to the laws of fluid dynamics, adjacent water masses of different densities will tend to move relative to one another, following courses shaped by the spinning of the earth. The equations of the dynamical method — published in 1909 by two Scandinavian oceanographers — predicted what that movement would be from the temperature and salinity of the water masses involved. But no attempt to calculate the currents that gave rise to the distribution of deepwater properties charted by the *Meteor* scientists yielded conclusive results until the advent of a sophisticated new approach, some 30 years after the expedition.

In the mid-1950s, oceanographer Henry Stommel of the Woods Hole Oceanographic Institution announced a dynamical analysis that took into account a third dimension of water motion: the slow, upward mixing of water from the ocean depths into the surface layers. Complex considerations of the effects of the earth's rotation, he said, indicated that a layer of deep water continually losing mass through upward diffusion would tend to move poleward — a conclusion that seemed to contradict two centuries of observations that the source of the cold water in the depths lies in polar seas. But Stommel's further calculations as he developed his hypothesis indicated that, although deep water is creeping toward the Poles across most of the ocean floor, a deep flow originating at the Poles and coursing toward the Equator also exists, compensating for the poleward drift. It occurs, he

A Norwegian ship plows through pack ice in the Weddell Sea, off Antarctica. The winter freezing of the sea concentrates salt in the underlying water, contributing to the exceptionally high density that causes frigid Weddell surface water to subside into the ocean depths.

said, "in strong currents along the western sides of the ocean basins, just as there are strong currents along these routes at the ocean surface." Stommel termed these swift, concentrated flows of deep water deep western boundary currents.

In a reversal of the usual practice in science, Stommel's theory was an attempt not to explain data that had already been collected but to predict phenomena that had not yet been observed. Until the mid-1950s, direct measurements of subsurface currents were practically impossible because of the difficulty of accurately gauging and compensating for the movement of the ships from which instruments were suspended. The complicated dynamical method Stommel used to make his predictions had been developed as a substitute for direct observations of water in motion. But he did not have to wait long for confirmation; instruments and techniques of oceanographic research were advancing in lock step with theoretical progress.

In 1955, John Swallow of England's National Institute of Oceanography perfected a simple but invaluable device, a neutral-buoyancy float that came to be known as the Swallow float. At great depths, the pressure of the overlying ocean compresses sea water slightly, rendering it more dense. An object that is slightly denser than water at the sea surface will sink to the depth at which its density equals that of the surrounding water, providing the object itself is not compressed by the pressure of the deep, and will hover there. Swallow's floats were paired 10-foot lengths of sealed aluminum tubing, which is rigid enough to resist compression even at great depth. By means of careful ballasting, the floats could be sent to predetermined depths, where they would hover and drift with any existing current.

Each float was equipped with a battery-powered acoustic transmitter that emitted a ping every few seconds. For several days, until the batteries ran down, scientists on board ship could follow the float drifting in the depths by using hydrophones — submerged listening devices — to gauge the direction of the acoustic pings. But to establish the float's exact location and course, the tracking ship had to be able to fix its own position precisely — and that was made possible by a new aid to navigation that was one of many technical innovations bequeathed to oceanography by World War II. Called loran, which stands for "long range navigation," the system used specially broadcast radio signals to pinpoint within one quarter of a mile the location of a ship at sea.

Stommel had predicted the existence of a deep boundary current underneath the Gulf Stream in the mid-1950s; in March 1957, a joint British-American expedition equipped with the new Swallow floats rendezvoused in Bermuda. The two research vessels — the ketch *Atlantis* from Woods Hole and Britain's *Discovery II,* with Swallow and Stommel aboard — set a course for an area off the Carolinas at the eastern edge of the Gulf Stream. On the *Discovery's* deck, Swallow assembled and cast over the side seven of his long aluminum floats, each ballasted to sink to a different depth. The first few, set to hover at depths of 6,500 feet or less, sent back pings that indicated that they, like the watching research vessels, were coasting northward with the familiar flow of the Gulf Stream. But others, weighted to sink to 9,000 feet, drifted steadily southward at speeds of up to eight miles a day. The floats were traveling with the strongest flow of water ever recorded in the ocean depths — Stommel's theory of deep western boundary currents was resoundingly confirmed.

By 1970, either by tracking Swallow floats or by applying the dynamical method of current calculation, oceanographers had discovered worldwide counterparts to the southward-flowing boundary current that Stommel and Swallow had detected in the North Atlantic. Coursing northward from Antarctic seas rather than southward from the Arctic, the deep currents were traced along the western edges of the South Atlantic, Pacific and Indian Oceans. The outlines of the grand global pattern of deepwater circulation, with swift boundary currents carrying deep water away from polar sources, compensating for the theorized poleward creep across the rest of the ocean floor, had been established.

The driving force of this global circulation is surprisingly subtle: the action of gravity on tiny differences in water density. Throughout most of the ocean, density differences arising from varying temperatures and salinity cause water masses to arrange themselves in layers, with the densest water in the greatest depths, progressively lighter water above. But the differences in temperature and salinity among the layers in this watery hierarchy are minute. In the South Atlantic, for instance, the average water temperature 3,000 feet down is about 39° F., while at 13,000 feet it is

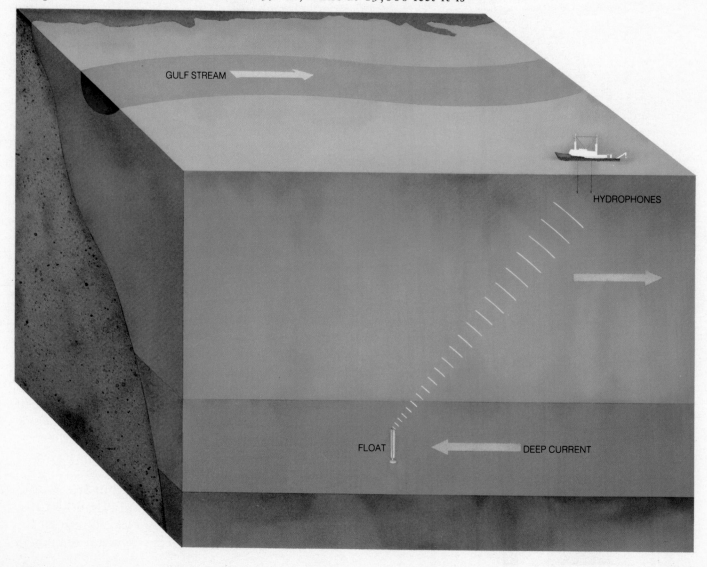

GULF STREAM

HYDROPHONES

FLOAT   DEEP CURRENT

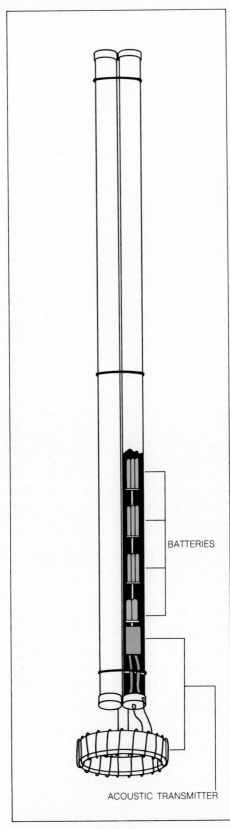

BATTERIES

ACOUSTIC TRANSMITTER

The first device designed to follow the currents of the ocean depths, the Swallow float (*above*) consists of twin 10-foot aluminum tubes. One is weighted for adjustable buoyancy, the other contains batteries for the ring-shaped transmitter with which scientists track the float. The illustration at left shows how, in 1957, Swallow floats in 9,000 feet of water off South Carolina were tracked southward, counter to the northerly flow of the Gulf Stream.

34° F. — cooler, hence denser, but not by much. The variation in salt content, and thus in density attributable to increased salinity, is even smaller: The proportion of salt increases from 34.5 parts per thousand at 3,000 feet to 34.8 at 13,000 feet.

Yet the layered structure engendered by these tiny variations is so stable in most of the world's oceans (beneath a surface layer, at most a few hundred feet thick, that is continually stirred by weather and the daily cycle of heating and cooling) that the deep layers of the ocean, like the stagnant upper reaches of the atmosphere, have been referred to as a stratosphere. Throughout most of the ocean, water masses simply hover at their respective density levels, circulating horizontally but mixing upward and downward with imperceptible slowness. But there is one crucial exception: In a few polar seas, unusually saline surface water and the harsh polar climate combine to produce cold surface water masses so dense that they sink deep into the ocean.

This sinking — known as thermohaline circulation because it is impelled by differences in water temperature and salinity — powers the deep movement of water toward the Equator first postulated by Count Rumford in the late 18th Century. In the depths of the polar seas, cold, salty water sinking from the surface displaces the bottom water, squeezing it outward along levels of constant water density, where its lateral movement is modified by the topography of the ocean bottom and deflected by the earth's rotation. The greatest single source of bottom water is the Weddell Sea, a large indentation in the coast of Antarctica directly south of the Atlantic Ocean. At the surface of this small, obscure corner of the oceans, harsh weather and peculiarities of surface flow create the densest ocean water in the world, highly saline and several degrees below the freezing point of fresh water. The Weddell Sea, in the words of one oceanographer, "is literally a factory of cold water."

The high salinity of Weddell Sea surface water is a consequence of sea ice formation. As sea water freezes, salt is excluded from the crystalline structure of the ice; pack ice consists of nearly fresh water, with the rejected salt concentrated in pockets of liquid brine within the ice. As the ice ages, the brine trickles from the floes into the sea water beneath, increasing the water's salinity and density. In many polar seas, water salinity peaks in winter, after the formation of sea ice, then is reduced in summer as the ice pack breaks up and melts. But the prevailing winds of the Weddell Sea drive the melting floes seaward, leaving the high-salinity waters above the continental shelf undiluted by meltwater.

Meanwhile, harsh winds from the Antarctic interior chill the shelf water to temperatures as low as 30° F., further increasing its density. The result is a continuous process of subsidence along the margins of the Weddell Sea. Sliding northward down the continental shelf, the erstwhile surface water sinks into the deep sea, mixing with warmer but also highly saline water as it passes through the middle depths. Ultimately, the combined water mass arrives at the floor of the Weddell Sea, at depths of up to 13,000 feet. There it joins the deep circulation that will channel it toward the Equator and, ultimately, back to Antarctic seas, thus forming the layer of Antarctic Bottom Water that carpets the greatest depths of much of the world's oceans.

Antarctic seas are the scene of other water displacements as well. As chill surface water sinks into the depths, deep-seated warmer water wells up to replace it. And farther from the Antarctic continent, at a latitude of about 50° S., another shift in the vertical hierarchy occurs. There, in a region known as the Antarctic Polar Front, surface water is of low salinity because of heavy snowfalls and melting pack ice. Driven northward by prevailing winds, this water encounters saltier and considerably warmer water moving southward from temperate latitudes. The temperature change at the Polar Front is so pronounced that one explorer returning from the Antarctic vividly remembered crossing "the line to the north of which we felt one day, at the right season, genial air again and soft rain like English rain in the spring."

The Antarctic surface water is close to the freezing point, and therefore is considerably more dense than the temperate water masses, which may be as warm as 60° F. Thus the northbound water sinks beneath the warmer masses at the zone of convergence and continues its northward progress at a depth of about 3,000 feet. This is the layer of Antarctic Intermediate Water — recognizable because of its low salinity — that was first charted in the 1920s by the *Meteor* expedition.

The Antarctic Bottom Water embarks on a much longer journey. Some of the water, newly arrived from the surface, circulates eastward around Antarctica. But much of it flows directly northward from the Weddell Sea into the western South Atlantic. Concentrated in the narrow boundary current predicted by Stommel's theory, it hugs the South American coast as far as the Equator, then, for reasons still unexplained, jogs eastward and follows the mountainous spine at the center of the Atlantic, the Mid-Atlantic Ridge. By the time it reaches the latitude of Cuba, the bottom current has become so depleted of its burden of chill water by being mixed with overlying warmer water layers and by the slow poleward flux of bottom water that occurs across the entire width of the ocean basin, that it is difficult to recognize.

In the North Atlantic, the flow of bottom water is dominated by the southward-flowing current, first detected in 1957 with deep-diving Swallow floats, that skirts North America's east coast. This southward boundary current channels water from the second great source of bottom water, the Norwegian Sea, between Greenland and Norway. There, as in the Weddell Sea, surface waters of high salinity and extremes of weather combine to effect exceptional increases in the density of the water. The high salinity, paradoxically, is the result of distant equatorial climates, for the Norwegian Sea lies at the end of the Gulf Stream, which funnels water northward from the tropics, where surface salinity is increased by evaporation.

Sharply chilled by Arctic winters, the water sinks into the depths. But high sills, rising from the sea floor 2,500 feet below to within 1,500 feet of the surface, bar the three routes from the Norwegian Sea into the open Atlantic — the channels between Scotland and the Faeroe Islands, between the Faeroes and Iceland, and between Iceland and Greenland. While most of the cold water remains pent up within the Norwegian Sea, some spills over the sills, cascading down their southern slopes at speeds of more than three miles per hour, rivaling the velocity of the Gulf Stream. Turbulence generated by this rapid descent mixes water from intermediate Atlantic depths into the Norwegian Sea overflow, and the resulting water mass — the North Atlantic Deep Water charted by the *Meteor* expedition — is neither as cold nor as saline as is the bottom water of the Norwegian Sea. But it is still saltier than the Antarctic Bottom Water — a distinctive trait that enables scientists to trace it throughout its southward progress down the western margin of the Atlantic.

As it moves into the Southern Hemisphere, the southbound current encounters the northward flow of Antarctic Bottom Water near the Equator. But the waters do not mix; despite its saltiness the Atlantic flow is slightly less dense than the colder Antarctic current and overrides it, continuing its southward progress until it joins the great deepwater flow around Antarctica itself.

The Antarctic Circumpolar Current is exceptional among ocean currents because it extends from the surface all the way to the deep-sea floor. Driven to the east by the unrelenting westerly winds of the Southern Ocean — as the continuous swath of ocean surrounding Antarctica is known — the current girdles the continent. Its speed is relatively sluggish: no more than a mile per hour at the surface, one fifth of that in the depths. But its rate of flow, an estimated 200 million tons of water per second, is double that of the Gulf Stream and would be sufficient to fill the Great Lakes within two days. It is the sole means by which the dense bottom water that is chilled in the Weddell and Norwegian Seas at opposite ends of the Atlantic is distributed laterally around the globe, into the deep basements of the other great oceans.

Because neither the Indian nor the Pacific Ocean encompasses a region with the combination of climate and water characteristics necessary to cause surface water to subside, their patterns of deep circulation are far simpler than those of the Atlantic. In the Indian Ocean, bottom water swept around the southern nub of Africa by the Circumpolar Current flows northward in boundary currents that hug the east coast of Africa and the eastern flank of the ocean's central north-south ridge. Deep water creeps slowly southward elsewhere in the Indian Ocean, eventually rejoining the circumpolar flow.

In the Pacific, a boundary current peels off the Antarctic Circumpolar Current south of New Zealand and courses northward along the western edge of the broad abyssal plain, skirting the seamounts and island chains of the western Pacific; elsewhere in that ocean a slow return flow toward Antarctic waters is believed to dominate the circulation. Remarkably, the two classes of deep water remain distinguishable even in the Pacific, half a world away from their sources: Temperature and salinity profiles of deep Pacific waters show, riding in a subtle layer above the chill waters that originated in the Weddell Sea, the slightly warmer and saltier water that flows from the Norwegian Sea.

The global pageant of bottom-water circulation, set in motion by the subsidence of cold, salty water in polar seas, could not continue if the water thus drawn from the sun-warmed surfaces of the world's oceans were not ultimately returned to the surface to complete the cycle. That return flow is accomplished by the constant upward diffusion of the deep waters throughout the oceans, at a rate so slow that it has never been measured. It has been estimated, though, that a molecule of water in the deep ocean moves upward at an average pace of less than a yard a day.

At that languid rate of upward diffusion, the circulation of water into the depths and back to the surface again must proceed slowly. And one measure

113

of the ponderous pace of recirculation has been established: the age of the deep water, measured from the time it sank from the surface of its polar sea. The dating technique is based on the water's content of carbon 14, which is absorbed by water in contact with the atmosphere but steadily disappears from deep water through a measurable process of radioactive decay. According to a series of studies conducted in the 1970s, the deep waters of the Atlantic are about 300 years old, on the average. And the bottom water of the eastern Pacific, having circulated halfway around the globe and throughout the Pacific depths since its formation, last saw the light of day some 2,000 years ago.

Stately as it is, the global pattern of deepwater circulation is everywhere subject to local perturbations. The most notable is the intrusion, in the eastern North Atlantic, of an enormous tongue of extremely saline water that is also, at 55° F., substantially warmer than surrounding water. As a result of the combination of warmth and high salinity, the water is of intermediate density and hovers in a thin layer 4,000 feet down in the middle depths of the Atlantic. There, the anomalous characteristics of this well-defined water mass make it recognizable as much as 1,500 miles from its source — the Mediterranean Sea.

For centuries this infusion into the Atlantic from the Mediterranean was a secret. On the other hand, every navigator was aware of the flow from the Atlantic into the Mediterranean. Because of these strong incoming currents, the earliest mariners found it virtually impossible to row their galleys through the Strait of Gibraltar out into the Atlantic. Only by adding sails and waiting for favorable winds were the Phoenicians able to make regular voyages into the Atlantic beginning about 800 B.C. As recently as 1855, one skipper wrote in his log that not only he but nearly a thousand other captains were unable to sail out through the strait because the easterly current was so strong and the winds were either contrary or too light. Some of these vessels had been swinging at their anchors for more than a month, waiting for the winds to shift and drive them against a current that was running at speeds up to three miles an hour.

Meanwhile, early scientists puzzled over the Mediterranean's ability to absorb all this incoming water without rising. In the 17th Century the British mathematician John Greaves guessed that excess water poured back out into the Atlantic through some subterranean passage. Others considered the possibility of a subsurface outward current through the strait. In 1870 the British scientist William Carpenter managed to anchor his research vessel *Porcupine* in the rushing surface current long enough to send down a sea anchor attached by a cable to a small boat floating on the surface. The boat scarcely moved against the inrushing surface flow, confirming that there was indeed an outflowing current, about 1,300 feet beneath the surface and racing almost as fast as the incoming one. Carpenter also guessed what caused the phenomenon: water layers of differing densities within the Mediterranean.

Shimmering under the summer sun, swept by arid winds from the deserts of North Africa, the Mediterranean loses an enormous amount of water to evaporation. The loss of that water draws the influx from the Atlantic Ocean that races through the strait. Elsewhere in the Mediterranean, evaporation renders the surface water salty and dense. When winter weather cools

A simplified Pole-to-Pole cross-section of the Atlantic Ocean, from the continent of Antarctica to the Arctic Ocean, shows the density and movements of major deepwater masses. The deepest water flows from polar regions of subsidence, while a water layer of intermediate depth sinks and spreads north of Antarctica. Deep water returns to the sea surface near Antarctica and in a zone of upwelling at the Equator, caused by prevailing winds.

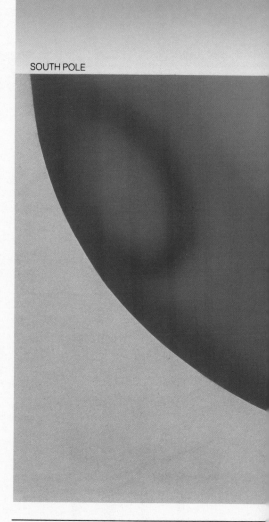

SOUTH POLE

114

Far beneath the turbulent domain of wind-driven currents on the surface, the deep ocean remains a place of unrest, where enormous masses of water circulate at all levels.

Many of the subsurface currents are set in motion by the sinking of the surface waters of remote polar seas, made dense by extreme cold and, often, by high salinity. The seas around Antarctica are the principal source of the deepest currents, because of the unique conditions of wind and surface currents found there and the presence of the climate-altering polar land mass.

In the Weddell Sea, near the Antarctic coast, cold and salty surface water sinks all the way to the ocean floor, driving abyssal currents that circle the globe and causing a compensating upsurge of deep water. Several hundred miles north of Antarctica, another region of cold but slightly less salty surface water subsides into the middle depths of the ocean, spurring a wide-ranging mid-level circulation.

Some of the deep water that wells up in the Weddell Sea comes from the other major source of deep currents, the Norwegian Sea, at the opposite end of the Atlantic between Greenland and Norway. Together, the currents of deep water flowing from the Weddell Sea and the Norwegian Sea web the floor of the entire world ocean with a pattern of circulation *(pages 116-117)* that is larger in geographic scope than any surface gyre. Flowing at depths of 10,000 feet and more, the abyssal currents generally are confined by an effect of the earth's rotation to the western sides of the ocean basins, although their paths are also shaped to some extent by the topography of the sea floor.

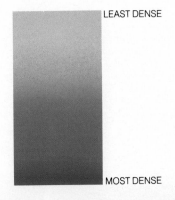

LEAST DENSE

MOST DENSE

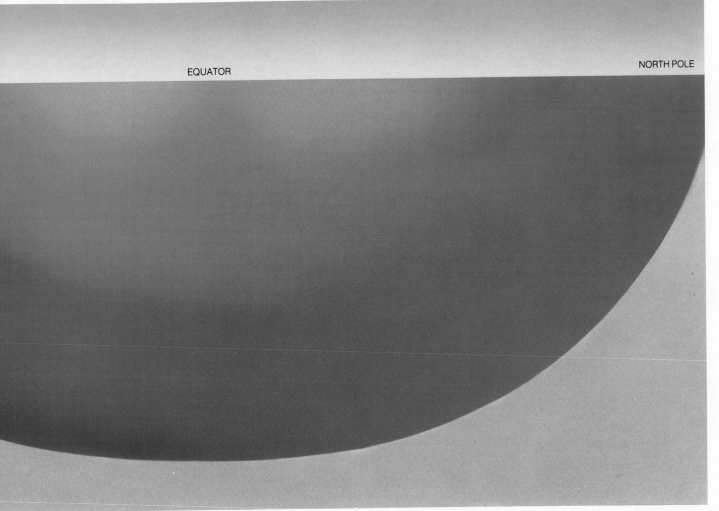

EQUATOR

NORTH POLE

Currents of deep water originating in the
Norwegian Sea *(red)* and in the Weddell Sea
(blue) web the floors of the world's oceans,
their paths determined by the spin of the earth
and the topography of the bottom. Although
wide-ranging, the abyssal currents are sluggish;
it takes centuries to circulate deep water
around the globe from its sources near the Poles.

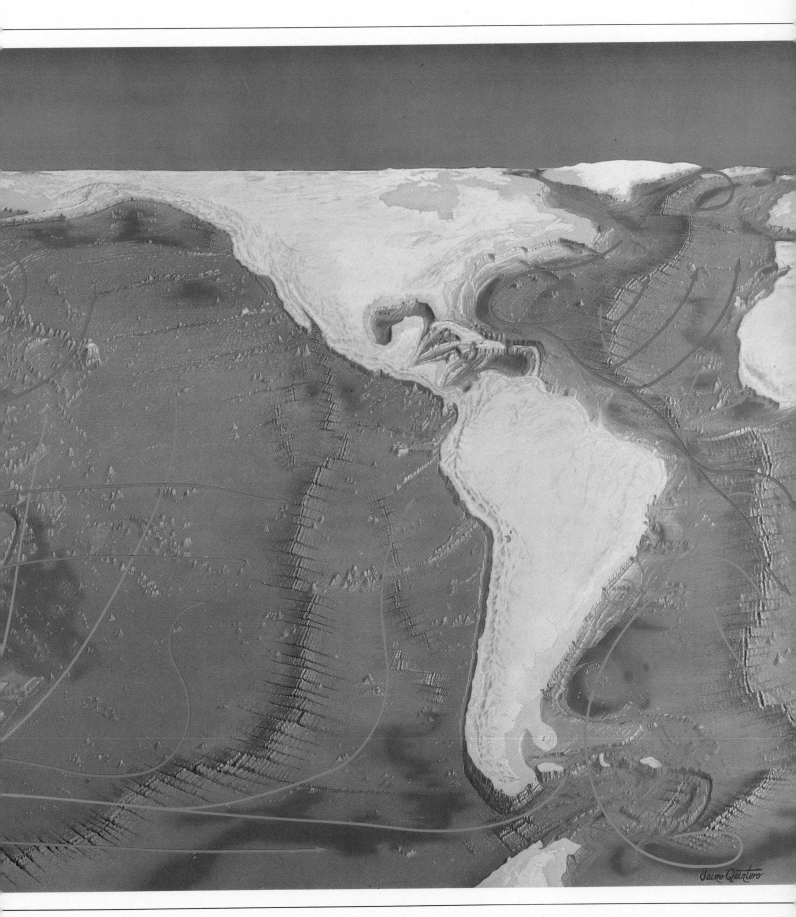

the water and further increases its density, it subsides. Flowing westward, this newly formed deep water eventually spills across the sill that spans the strait at a depth of 900 feet. Pouring over the barrier like a waterfall, the salty Mediterranean water slides down into the open Atlantic. Its velocity is such that it has scoured the sill down to bare rock, and it often smashes the current meters lowered to measure it. At a depth of 4,000 feet in the Atlantic, the density of the plunging Mediterranean water matches that of its surroundings, and it begins to spread horizontally into the stratified Atlantic.

Density differences also are responsible for a more violent perturbation of the deep sea, one that was not understood until recently. On November 18, 1929, a submarine earthquake rocked the Grand Banks, an area of shoals south of Newfoundland. Eight transatlantic telegraph cables near the epicenter of the quake snapped instantly. But during the next 13 hours five more cables, each progressively farther from the epicenter, snapped in sequence, the last one 500 miles distant in a deep basin of the North Atlantic. Eventually, oceanographers connected that puzzling event with two other mysteries. In 1947, the Woods Hole research ship *Atlantis* dredged from the ocean bottom hundreds of miles from shore, in the deepest part of the western Atlantic, sand and sediment identical to the ooze that carpets the continental shelf just off New England. Later, improved maps of the sea floor revealed features that resembled submerged river valleys, snaking for hundreds of miles beyond the continental shelf.

All three phenomena are believed to result from so-called turbidity currents — cascades of sediment-laden water — that occasionally race down the continental slope and across the abyssal floor. An earthquake or the undersea equivalent of a landslide, striking the sediment-blanketed continental slope, can stir vast quantities of silt into the overlying water. The burden of suspended particles sharply increases the density of the water, sending it spilling down the slope into the deepest parts of the abyss. Scientists think that the silty water mass of a turbidity current might reach speeds of 50 miles per hour and gain momentum enough to carry it far out onto the abyssal plain, creating deep-sea deposits of sediment, sculpting channels in the sea floor — and snapping any submerged cables that lie in its path.

But turbidity currents are by nature isolated events. A more pervasive disturbance in deepwater flow was discovered by the *Aries* expedition of 1959-1960. Using his ingenious floats, the British oceanographer John Swallow was seeking to vindicate Henry Stommel's prediction of a sluggish deepwater flow toward the Poles, balancing the deep western boundary currents that channel water away from high latitudes. In the waters off Bermuda, Swallow and his colleagues launched 30 floats, most of them ballasted to drift at depths between 6,600 and 13,000 feet, and tracked them for more than a year. The results were startling: Although the floats often showed a net progress to the north, their motions were anything but sluggish and steady. They scattered in every direction, looping and darting through the depths at speeds of up to 12 miles a day.

Scientists soon discovered that such erratic eddies are common throughout the oceans, both at the surface and in the depths, that individual eddies affect expanses of ocean tens to hundreds of miles across, and that they may endure for weeks or months before dissipating. But these energetic stirrings

Sampling bottles arrayed in an apparatus called a rosette are winched over the side of a Soviet research ship. As the instrument package descends into the depths, electronic sensors transmit continuous readings of the water's temperature and salinity, while the bottles, tripped by remote control at various depths, capture samples for later analysis.

remain fraught with mysteries—among them, the source of the underwater whirlpools' energy and their relation to the steady currents of the surface and the depths.

Eddies became a central focus of oceanographic investigations during the 1970s. Because individual eddies are relatively small compared with the expanse of an ocean, their study called for densely spaced measurements gathered through more efficient techniques of deep-sea research. One advance was an improved version of the Swallow float. Called a "sofar" (for "sound fixing and ranging") float, the new device does not need to be tracked by a ship following at close range. Instead, large numbers of sofar floats can be monitored simultaneously—distinguished by the differing frequencies and rates of their sonic pings.

Sofar floats were an essential tool in the eddy investigations of the Mid-Ocean Dynamics Experiment (MODE) of 1973, which studied eddy motions in a 400-mile swath of ocean between Florida and Bermuda. In addition to the floats, scientists used an array of sophisticated current meters, moored at depths of up to 13,000 feet, that electronically recorded the varying speeds and directions of water motion over a period of several months. Similar techniques were used in the 1977-1978 successor to MODE, a joint United States-Soviet endeavor called POLYMODE that studied eddies across a broader area of the North Atlantic.

Other investigations detailed the effects of eddies on the sediment carpet of the ocean floor. An instrument package called Deep Tow has been a crucial tool in such studies; drawn behind a surface ship, it skims the deep-sea floor and scans the bottom contours with sonar and a stereoscopic camera. Deep Tow's photographs and readings have shown that the sediment blanket of much of the deep ocean is patterned with undulations, ranging from inch-long ripples to ridges tens of feet high with crests several miles apart.

It is likely that much of this muddy topography has been sculpted by the steady flow of bottom water, especially the swift western boundary currents. But some of the sea-floor tracings seem to be the result of particularly strong eddies that swirl into the ocean depths and stir up sediments in what have been called benthic storms. In the deep ocean off Cape Cod, where the phenomenon has been studied most intensively, benthic storms seem to strike any given site on the ocean floor three to five times a year. They are so powerful that, as observed by underwater cameras, bottom water for hundreds of feet above the sea floor grows completely opaque with suspended sediment, in the abyssal equivalent of a blizzard.

Future eddy studies may depend on a new technique that takes advantage of an ocean characteristic known for centuries: that the sea is as transparent to sound as the atmosphere is to light. Perhaps the first to note this singular fact was the 15th Century genius Leonardo da Vinci, who wrote: "If you cause your ship to stop, and place the head of a long tube in the water, and place the other extremity to your ear, you will hear ships at great distances." Although the sea is a consummately hospitable medium for sound, the speed of undersea sound varies with the temperature and salinity of the water masses through which it passes.

And, as Scandinavian oceanographers discovered early in the 20th Century, variations in sea-water temperature and salinity are the hallmark of water motions. It should thus be possible to detect currents and eddies through the behavior of sound in the deep sea. In 1979, two oceanographers, Walter Munk of Scripps and Carl Wunsch of the Massachusetts Institute of Technology, proposed an acoustic technique by which scientists could measure water motions within vast areas of ocean far more quickly and efficiently than ever before. By arraying sound transmitters and receivers, moored at mid-depths, along the boundaries of the study area, investigators could crisscross the intervening ocean with sound pulses, each following a slightly different path. The variations in travel time, interpreted by computer, would yield an accurate map of water properties — and thus of the eddying currents stirring the depths.

Called ocean acoustic tomography, the method was tested in a 1981 experiment in which four sound transmitters were ranged opposite five receivers 180 miles away. Moored at a depth of 6,500 feet, the instruments exchanged sound pulses while investigators gathered data for com-

Subsurface internal waves etch the Gulf of California at concentric intervals of up to a mile and a quarter. Normally invisible, the waves were captured by a satellite radar image that recorded the bands of still and ruffled surface water spawned by the deep-seated movement.

parison with conventional current meters and instrument-carrying ships. The data received from the acoustic array indicated eddies precisely where the conventional techniques had located them—and the tomographic concept was vindicated.

Subsurface water motions remained obscure for so long because they have little or no effect on mariners. But there is one notable exception. Since the earliest days of seafaring, sailors have reported instances in which, for no apparent reason, a ship would suddenly lose headway despite strong oarsmen, stiff breezes or a good head of steam. In classical times, it was believed that a small sucker fish called a remora, occasionally found clinging to a keel, could exert magical powers on a ship. In one story related by the Roman historian Pliny, the Emperor Caligula's progress was rudely interrupted when one of the galleys in his fleet appeared to be rooted to a single spot in the deep ocean. But when the crew dislodged a remora found sticking to the rudder of the galley, the errant ship could once again be rowed. In later centuries, mariners faced with the same vexing phenomenon often attempted to break free by assaulting the water with oars, handspikes or gunfire; by sprinkling oil on the sea surface; or by ordering the entire crew to run fore and aft on deck, violently rocking the ship.

Such "dead-water" is especially common in the fjords and ice-clogged seas of Scandinavia. The oceanographer Fridtjof Nansen was himself once caught in dead-water as his research ship, the *Fram*, approached a region of pack ice. The schooner "made hardly any way, in spite of the engine going at full pressure," wrote Nansen. "In spite of the *Fram's* weight, and the momentum she usually has, we could in the present instance go at full speed till within a fathom or two of the edge of the ice, and hardly feel a shake when she touched." Yet it was not Nansen but the versatile Swedish oceanographer V. W. Ekman who finally explained the ancient puzzle.

Ekman knew that fjord waters are characterized by pronounced layering: A thin sheet of fresh water, discharged by rivers and released by melting sea ice, floats above the salty, denser water of the open sea. Just as waves form where water encounters less-dense air, they can occur at the boundary between water layers of different densities. He reasoned that if a ship's keel were to slice through a thin surface layer of light water to the denser water beneath, its motion might create a train of submerged waves along the border between the two water types. These so-called internal waves would tend to travel slowly, at no more than one or two miles an hour. Their effect on a ship would be to limit the vessel's speed to that of the wave train it had set in motion: As the ship tried to accelerate, the energy of its sails, oars or propeller would be siphoned off, contributing to the amplitude of the internal waves rather than to the craft's forward motion. The ship would break free only when it sailed clear of the layered surface water.

To verify his guess, Ekman built a glass-walled tank in his laboratory, filled it with layers of water of different salinities—with each layer dyed a different color for observation—and towed a model ship across this simulated fjord. Beneath the surface ripples that trailed behind the model, the cause of dead-water became apparent as sets of submerged waves appeared, corrugating the boundaries between the density layers and exerting a powerful drag on the toy ship.

Living evidence of internal waves, planktonic crab larvae stripe the sea surface off the coast of New Zealand. Spaced about 90 feet apart, the accumulations of crimson larvae mark zones of converging surface water that occur between adjacent internal waves.

Internal waves are now known to affect levels of the ocean far below the depth of a ship's keel. They not only move along the horizontal boundaries between stratified water layers at any depth, reaching amplitudes of 300 feet and wavelengths of several miles, but they can also travel vertically, along the density boundary between water masses circulating side by side. Unlike most deepwater motions, internal waves are often visible at the sea surface. When they pass within several hundred feet of the surface, these enormous undulations foster subtle movements of the surface water that cause glassy, ripple-free bands to form parallel to, but just behind, the submerged wave crests. Because these slicks mark zones of convergence, where surface water is gently gathered together by the ponderous water motions below, they tend to accumulate bands of floating detritus — trash, seaweed, even plankton — that provide shipboard observers with telltale markers of the submerged stirrings.

Most modern ships move too quickly to be ensnared by these internal waves. But the slight variations in water density that pattern the ocean are of crucial importance to submarines — which must deal directly with the phenomena of the deep sea. To maintain its depth, a submarine must remain in equilibrium with the density of the sea water surrounding it. Even a slight change in water salinity or temperature can alter the buoyancy of a submarine by several tons, deflecting it upward or downward. By filling or draining ballast tanks of sea water, submariners can compen-

FLIP abandons its guise as a conventional ship *(top left)* as its bow rises from the waves *(center left)*, lofted by the sinking stern section, and crew members brace themselves on an outside platform *(lower left)*. Bristling with instrument booms, winches and antennas *(above)*, FLIP may remain in working position for several weeks, while its crew occupies quarters that are made habitable by such adaptable amenities as dual washbasins *(right)*.

The Ship That Dives for Science

Scientists making observations from the decks of ships that are rocked by waves and wind are often prevented from detecting the ocean's subtler dynamics. But one unlikely craft called FLIP — an acronym that stands for Floating Instrument Platform — transcends the limitations of shipboard research.

Built in 1962 for the Scripps Institution of Oceanography, FLIP is an unpowered vessel that rides horizontally, drawing less than 15 feet of water. When the craft has been towed to its research site, sometimes as far from its home berth in San Diego as the Caribbean, the crew floods the ballast tanks in the cigar-shaped hull. Within 20 minutes, a 300-foot length of hull sinks, stern first, hoisting the 55-foot bow section into a new incarnation as a vertical, four-tiered floating laboratory.

The vertical FLIP, its stern rooted in the calm water of the depths, is, in the words of one observer, "almost as stable as a fencepost." The 30-foot swells of one severe storm caused it to bob no more than three feet. From this imperturbable vantage point, oceanographers have conducted precise studies of such transient and small-scale phenomena as underwater sound and internal waves.

sate for gradual density changes, and thus maintain a constant depth. But if a submarine operating near its maximum safe depth suddenly encountered an internal wave that enveloped the craft in a trough of lighter water, it might sink to a hull-crushing depth before the crew could restore its buoyancy.

The influence of the ocean's layers on underwater sound affects submarines in another vital way. Because neither light nor radar can penetrate the dense ocean very far, surface ships detect submarines with sound, which travels great distances underwater. By the middle years of World War I, Allied merchantmen and their escorts were using crude listening devices to detect German U-boats. And within a few years a new kind of detection system was designed to seek out a submarine, even after it had shut down its engines and was hovering soundlessly in the depths. Now known as sonar, the system locates a submerged object by emitting sound pulses and detecting echoes returning from the object, determining its position by the hearing and time delay of the echoes.

Since water is transparent to sound, it would seem that sonar leaves a submarine with no place to hide. But the travels of sound in the sea are by no means direct. Underwater sound travels at average speeds of about 3,350 miles per hour — more than four times faster than sound in the atmosphere. But its velocity varies with the properties of the water through which it passes, increasing in water of higher temperature, salinity or pressure. As a sound wave passes between water masses in which those properties differ, it is bent, or refracted, toward the water in which sound travels more slowly. The same phenomenon bends light rays passing from air into water, and is analogous to the tendency of a car, straddling the edge of a road, to veer off the pavement and into the dirt, the medium that slows its travel.

Water pressure increases steadily with depth everywhere in the ocean, and salinity variations in the open ocean are usually too small to influence the travel of underwater sound significantly. But the other factor affecting sound refraction — temperature — is subject to wide variations in the uppermost layers of the ocean according to the location, season and time of day. In certain water-temperature patterns, some of the sound waves from a sonar generator may be reflected upward while others are refracted downward into denser water, creating a so-called shadow zone (page 127), in which a submerged submarine might be undetectable by the sonar of a ship less than a mile away. Under the same temperature conditions, however, sonar pulses broadcast into the depths often are refracted back toward the surface layers of the ocean 30 miles away, making the same submarine vulnerable to deep-diving sound pulses from a distant, powerful sonar source.

Because water temperatures drop rapidly with depth, beginning just below the sea surface, the velocity of undersea sound falls to a minimum of about 3,320 miles per hour at a depth that varies between 2,000 and 4,000 feet. Below that level, water temperature decreases more slowly, the effect of increasing water pressure becomes predominant and sound velocity increases again. Refraction operates to bend sound traveling both in deeper and shallower layers toward the middle zone of slowest sound velocity; a sound wave can become trapped along this depth, following an undulating path for thousands of miles through the middle depths of the ocean.

So efficient is this deep sound channel that, during a 1960 experiment, the sound of depth charges fired off Australia was detected off Bermuda by hydrophones suspended in the depths. The interval between the detonations and the detected sound pulse was three and one half hours — the time it took the sound to traverse 12,000 miles of ocean. Like every other aspect of deep-sea sound behavior, the deep sound channel has military importance: Sensitive hydrophones moored at the velocity minimum could pick up mechanical noises from submarines hundreds or even thousands of miles distant.

Military uses of undersea sound are complicated not only by the properties of sea water, but also by the living creatures of the sea. Sonar and hydrophone operators must contend with the acoustic static produced as schools of shrimp snap their claws, the deceptively mechanical grindings and thumpings from such evocatively named fish as croakers and drumfish (one of which was once mistaken for a submarine transmitting an international distress signal), and submarine-sized echoes from the flanks of whales. But the largest single acoustic phenomenon of undersea life — and the greatest source of consternation to sonar operators — is the product of schools of small, silent fish, crustaceans, and jellyfish-like creatures called siphonophores spread thinly through the ocean depths.

Together, these unexceptional creatures constitute the deep scattering layers, so named for their remarkable effect on sonar. Their existence first came to light during World War II, when physicists aboard the U.S.S. *Jasper,* experimenting with sonar systems in the deep Pacific off the coast of San Diego in 1942, noted that their sonar pings regularly returned from a depth of scarcely 1,000 feet, as if they were reflected from an undersea surface. Nor was the phenomenon an isolated anomaly: The crew of the *Jasper* traced the phantom bottom across 300 miles of ocean. Later findings compounded the mystery: Several ghostly surfaces often could be detected layered one above another within the same area of ocean, each reflecting sonar energy from a different depth. Their source was unknown, but their military significance as a possible camouflage for deep-diving submarines was clear, and the discovery of the layers was immediately classified as a military secret.

By the end of the War, scientists had noted characteristics of the deep scattering layers that hinted at their origin in schools of small, mobile sea creatures. Sonar echoes returning from the layers were diffuse, suggesting widely dispersed objects, rather than sharp, as from an abrupt physical boundary. But most telling of all was the fact that the layers seemed to make a daily migration: During the day, they were detectable at depths of 700 to 2,400 feet, but at dusk, they rose to within a few feet of the surface. At the first light of dawn, they plunged at a rate of 25 feet per minute back to their former depth. And as the layers rose and fell, the pitch of the echoes changed, suggesting that the sonar pulses were reflecting from the swim bladders of fish or from gas bubbles enclosed in simpler marine creatures, such as siphonophores: In the course of a vertical journey, a gas bladder or bubble would change in size — and thus in resonant frequency — in response to changes in water pressure.

At night, the organisms of the deep scattering layers merge with the teeming life of surface waters and cannot be distinguished. But they have been identified, during the daytime, by direct observation from deep-sea

The diagram above shows how certain water conditions cause sound rays to diverge, creating a so-called shadow zone where a submarine cannot be detected by a surface ship's sonar. In well-mixed surface waters *(green layer),* conditions of constant water temperature and rising pressure cause sound speed to increase with depth. Because sound waves bend away from zones of increasing sound velocity, all but the most steeply angled sound rays veer back toward the surface. In deeper water *(blue layer),* temperature falls rapidly with depth, causing sound speed to decrease and the sonar beams to bend more sharply downward. In the deepest waters *(dark blue),* water properties once again make sound bend upward.

submersibles and from the few specimens captured in towed nets (concentrations of deep scattering layer animals are surprisingly low, ordinarily no more than one to five creatures per cubic yard of water). The cause of their daily migration, however, remains a mystery. It is clear that light triggers the swift vertical movement; during the daytime, a deep scattering layer monitored by sonar was seen to rise briefly as a passing cloud dimmed the sun. Some scientists think that this responsiveness to light allows the small, defenseless animals of the layers to take advantage of the rich food reserves in the surface layers of the ocean without suffering heavy predation: By rising for food only at night, then sinking into the sunless depths before daylight, the tiny creatures remain invisible to attackers.

The productive regions of the ocean that attract the deep scattering layer animals lie several miles above the oceanic levels affected by deep circulation. Yet the ecology of ocean life is profoundly influenced by the immensities of water yawning beneath this surface-water habitat — and by the obscure stirrings taking place in the depths.

The creatures of the deep scattering layers, despite their vertical mobility, have little control over their lateral movements and tend to drift with surface currents. Along with the other living flotsam of the sea, they are known as plankton. And it is with another group of marine drifters, the microscopic plants known as phytoplankton, that the food web of the ocean begins.

On land, the basic food-producing process of photosynthesis, by which the energy of sunlight is used to convert water and carbon dioxide gas into sugars, takes place in green plants of all sizes, some of them many times the size of the animals that browse on them. But in the open ocean, where large plants are rare, the size of an organism and its position in the food web are closely matched, and microscopic phytoplankton, which directly and indi-

A school of silvery mackerel flashes through the life-rich surface waters of the Pacific Ocean off the California coast. Mackerel occupy an intermediate

rank in the oceanic food web: A scourge of smaller fish such as herring, they are in turn eaten by tuna and swordfish.

rectly nourish all other life in the ocean, are the tiniest — albeit the most abundant — of marine life forms.

The phytoplankton are restricted to the uppermost layers of the ocean by their need for sunlight to perform photosynthesis; the greatest depth at which they are found varies from perhaps 100 feet in turbid coastal waters to 325 feet in the clearest tropical oceans. As a result, the animal life of the sea also congregates in the surface layers.

One step removed from the primary food production of the marine plants are the zooplankton, the drifting animals that include most of the creatures of the deep scattering layer. Many of the zooplankton are microscopic, but this group of drifters also includes shrimp and other crustaceans, larval forms of larger marine animals, worms, shell-less snails, and jellyfish trailing tentacles many feet long. Smaller zooplankton feed on the tiny planktonic plants, using sievelike mouth parts or sticky secretions to snag their meals. Others live by preying on fellow zooplankton.

At the highest levels of the food web are large, free-swimming predators — fish, squid, dolphins, seals and whales — that roam the ocean under their own power, more or less independent of winds and currents. These strong, specialized swimmers are known as the nekton, and they too are enmeshed in a hierarchy of predator and prey. Thus, plankton-eating herring are eaten by fish such as tarpon and tuna, which in turn fall prey to sharks. In general, the higher a species ranks in the food web, the sparser its population, for the transfer of nourishment from prey to predator is inefficient: It takes roughly 10 pounds of phytoplankton to nurture a pound of zooplankton and 10 pounds of zooplankton to produce a pound of herring — and the same rate of conversion continues to the highest levels of the food web.

Below the sunlit surface layers lies a chill, dark immensity of ocean that is at once the largest habitat on earth — comprising more than 78 per cent of the earth's habitable volume — and the most sparsely populated. In the inky depths, photosynthetic plants cannot exist, and nourishment enters this realm in another form: in a continuous rain of leavings — excrement and corpses — from the banquet above. Some food also arrives in the form of the animals of the deep scattering layer, which fall victim to the predators of the deep during their daytime retreat.

In this realm of darkness and famine, startling adaptations are the norm. Perhaps two thirds of the fish, crustaceans and squid of the depths produce biological light — to attract and illuminate prey, to confuse attackers, and perhaps to signal members of the same species. Some glow by activating specialized cells; others draw back flaps of skin to unveil symbiotic colonies of luminous bacteria living at the surface of their bodies. Although the bodies of abyssal fish are often weak and withered, requiring little nourishment, many deep-dwellers are equipped with enormous mouths and distensible stomachs that enable them to engulf any prey they encounter in the sparsely populated depths. Large eyes are common in creatures living at depths of up to 1,600 feet, where the last rays of daylight still glow dimly. But the eyes of creatures living in the total darkness below that depth have in many cases degenerated to pinpoint size.

Even at its surface, most of the ocean does not approach the biological productivity of the land. By one estimate, the average amount of organic matter produced each year beneath a given area of sea surface is less than

1/25 of that yielded by the same area of good farmland. This low fertility reflects the fundamental disadvantage of the ocean as an environment for life. On land, the organic compounds contained in excrement and dead plants and animals are released into the soil by processes of decay, ready for use by new generations. At sea, by contrast, organic wastes are lost to the depths, and life in the surface waters quickly exhausts available nutrients, with the result that vast areas of open ocean are virtual biological deserts. The storied blue of the Mediterranean and of tropical seas in fact betokens a sparse growth of plankton, high concentrations of which leave sea water murky and green. Marine life is most abundant in coastal waters, where rivers pour essential nutrients into the open sea, and in polar regions, where fierce storms frequently stir the ocean to great depths, driving sinking nutrients back to the surface.

But the greatest exceptions to the low fertility of the ocean occur in regions of upwelling deep water, where the nutrients lost from the sunlit surface layers at last return to the surface. Upwelling is often driven by prevailing winds or by surface currents. But the greatest zone of upwelling, nurturing the most spectacular assemblage of marine life, results from the ponderous exchange of surface and deep waters taking place in the Antarctic seas.

Ceaselessly supplied with nutrients by deep water welling up to replace the chilly, salty surface water sinking to the sea floor, the 12 million square miles of the Southern Ocean host an unparalleled abundance of phytoplankton. These marine pastures in turn nourish zooplankton, primarily two-inch shrimplike creatures called krill, in concentrations of up to 36 pounds per cubic yard of surface water — a density of living matter that, across the immensity of the Southern Ocean, amounts to a biomass of perhaps five billion tons. The wealth of krill is fodder for 350,000 whales, tens of millions of seals and nearly 200 million sea birds — living evidence of the deep-seated water movements that stir the world's oceans. Ω

Workings of the Ocean Food Web

Ocean life varies less across horizontal distances of thousands of miles than it does within vertical spans of a few thousand feet. For, like the physical structure of the ocean, the life of the deep sea is stratified, existing in distinct but interrelated layers.

Nourishment for all ocean life originates in the sunlit surface layers, where microscopic plants called phytoplankton use carbon dioxide, dissolved minerals, and the energy of sunlight to synthesize food. Small fish and zooplankton — drifting creatures such as sea worms, jellyfish and crustaceans — browse on these minute plants, and the food value thus provided moves through successive steps of predation, up the marine food web to the largest sea dwellers.

Most of the zooplankton and the free-swimming ocean denizens known as the nekton — including the fish, squids and whales — congregate in the food-rich surface waters. But some animal life is found at all levels. Species such as flying fish even take to the air, temporarily, to elude attackers. Others, including lanternfish, migrate between different depths in search of food or haven from predators. Still others are permanent residents of the deepest waters.

The fish and crustaceans of the sunless depths are sustained by the organic debris — excrement and corpses — that drifts down from the fecund surface layers. Some feed directly on this secondhand nourishment; others, a step or two up the food web, prey on the scavengers.

Yet the deep dwellers do not snag all of the organic fallout, and they themselves loose a meager rain of detritus. Accumulating on the bottom, the debris is broken down by bacteria. Ultimately, many of the mineral nutrients thus released are swept to the surface again — often in coastal zones of upwelling — where they fuel the continuing growth of phytoplankton.

A diagram of the multilayered environment of the ocean arranges representative marine species according to their relative depths. Phytoplankton *(white stippling)* flourish only in surface waters but are dependent on minerals upwelling from the bottom *(arrow)*.

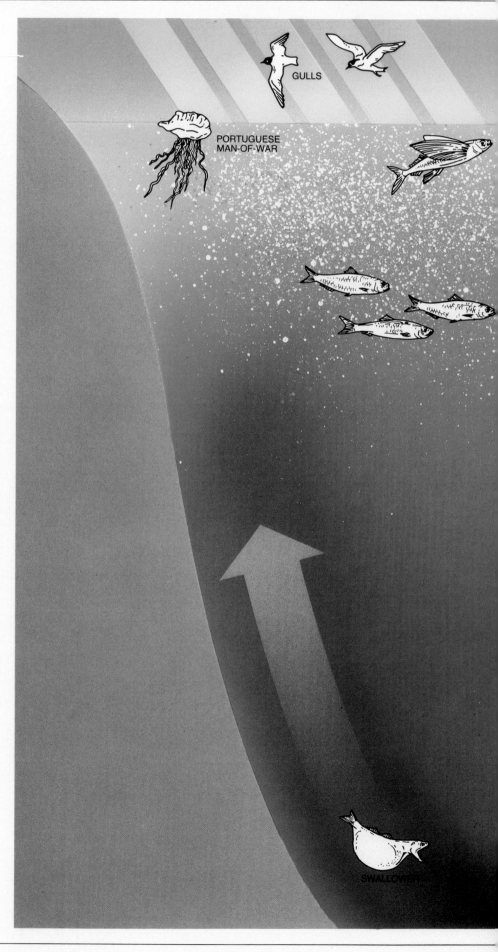

GULLS

PORTUGUESE MAN-OF-WAR

SWALLOWER

FLYING FISH

PELICAN

TUNA

DOLPHIN FISH

MACKEREL

HERRING

BLUE WHALE

BASKING
SHARK

SQUID

SPERM WHALE

LANTERNFISH

HATCHETFISH

DRAGONFISH

PRAWNS

VIPERFISH

ANGLERFISH

GULPER

Life beneath the waves has an aura of science fiction. Many of the denizens of the open ocean belong to classes of animals that lack the skeletons and much of the basic anatomy of higher forms and look more like abstract sculptures in protoplasm than living creatures. Moreover, their habits complement their otherworldly mien. Some spurt through the depths, propelled by a kind of biological jet power. Some species are linked in improbable symbiosis and macabre parasitic relationships. And many reproduce asexually, by mass-producing clones.

Most of these simple creatures, such as jellyfish, salps and crustaceans, are zooplankton — animals that either drift passively or swim weakly, but cannot in any case propel themselves against tides and currents. Many are fragile and diaphanous, able to survive only because of the utter absence of physical stresses in their ocean environment: They are buoyed by the enveloping sea water, isolated from hard surfaces and unruffled by water motions, just as a balloonist experiences a dead calm while riding with the wind.

Even the less ethereal, better-known sea creatures, such as fish and squids, often present startling visages; many glow with biological light, and some deep-water fish display fearsome adaptations for snaring prey in their sparsely populated domain.

Several of the marine animals on this and the following pages are portrayed in their open-ocean habitat. Others were captured by divers or trawled from the depths, then photographed aboard ship under the careful oblique lighting necessary to highlight their delicate outlines.

A planktonic starship skimmed from the sea surface, an inch-long prawn larva displays oarlike appendages that aid in flotation and, at far left, feathery antennae and protruding eyes.

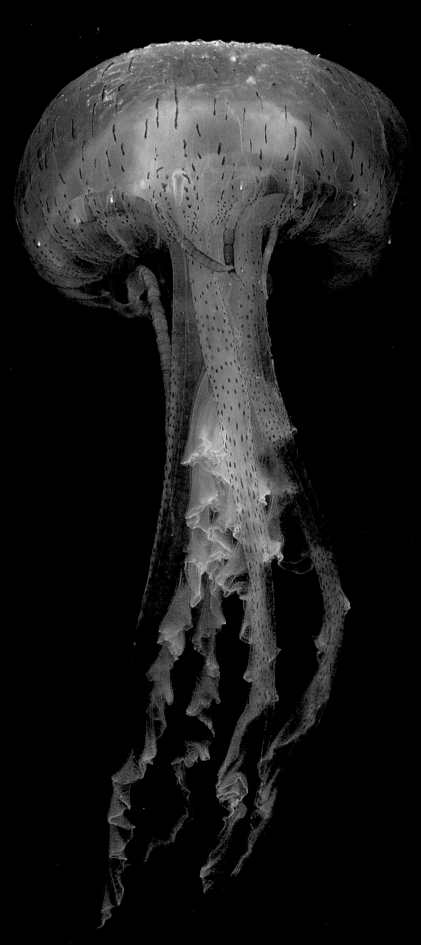

Photographed at a depth of 40 feet, a five-inch jellyfish trails frilly mouth openings and reddish stinging tentacles, here contracted but capable of extending seven feet.

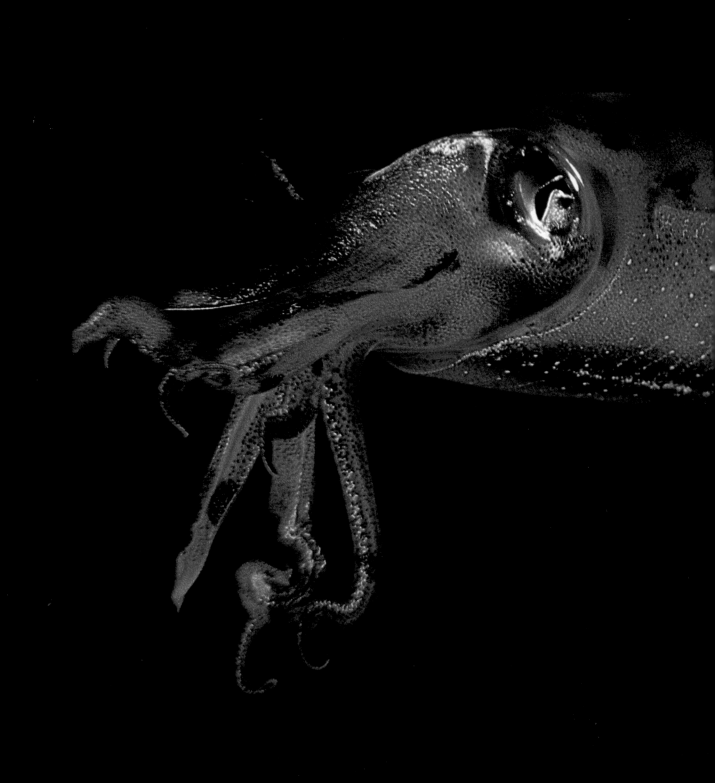

Spangled with light-producing organs called photophores, a 12-inch squid jets through the sea at night, propelled by pulses of water drawn into its body, then spurted from an opening on its underside. The photographer's flash glints in one of the animal's large, sensitive eyes.

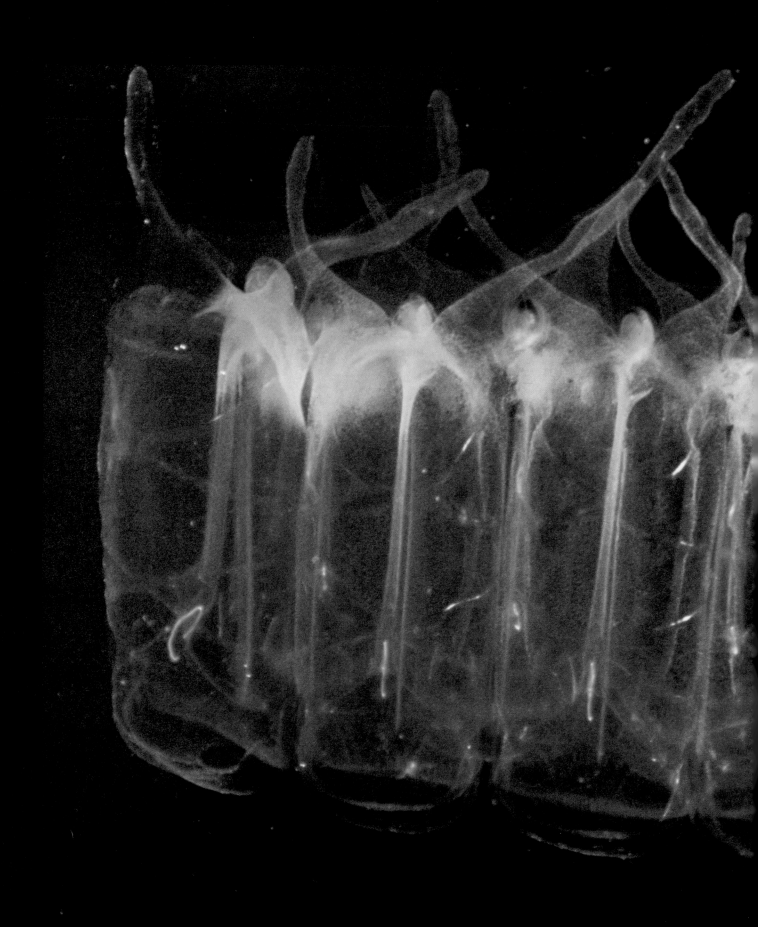

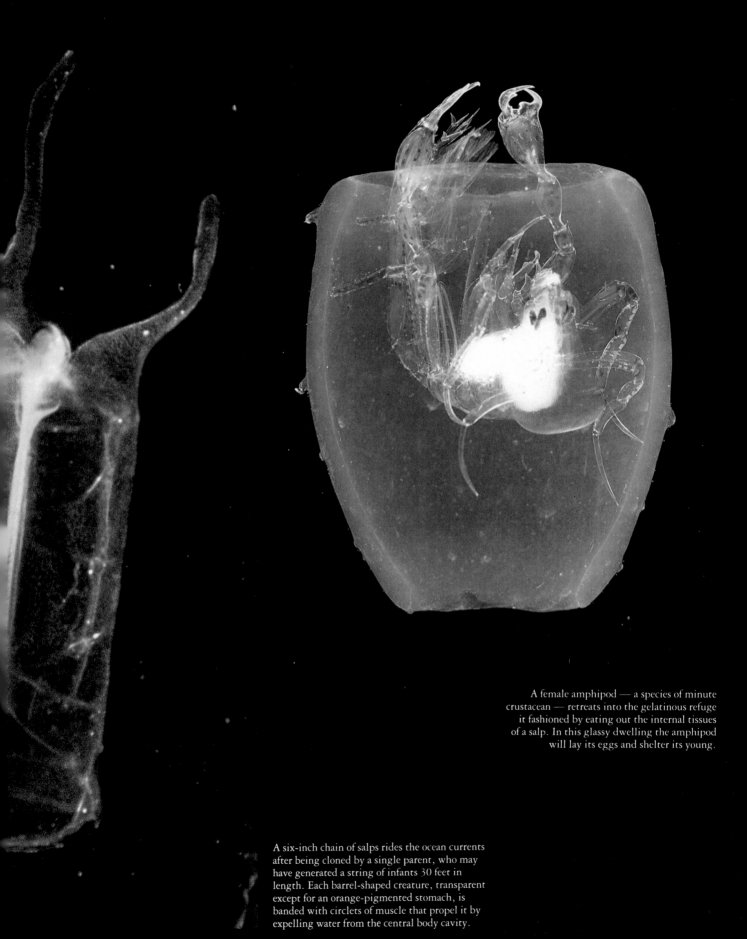

A female amphipod — a species of minute
crustacean — retreats into the gelatinous refuge
it fashioned by eating out the internal tissues
of a salp. In this glassy dwelling the amphipod
will lay its eggs and shelter its young.

A six-inch chain of salps rides the ocean currents
after being cloned by a single parent, who may
have generated a string of infants 30 feet in
length. Each barrel-shaped creature, transparent
except for an orange-pigmented stomach, is
banded with circlets of muscle that propel it by
expelling water from the central body cavity.

A 12-inch cat shark, trawled from a depth
of 1,800 feet, differs from its fearsome surface-
water relatives not only in its diminutive size
but also in its ability to survive in bottom waters
that are depleted of dissolved oxygen by
decaying organic matter. Scientists speculate
that the cat shark periodically rises to the
surface to refresh its system.

Menacing but minute, a six-inch anoplogaster,
netted several thousand feet down, displays
the traits of an abyssal fish: sooty coloration and
needle-like teeth that ensure that prey, rare in
the ocean depths, cannot slip free once captured.

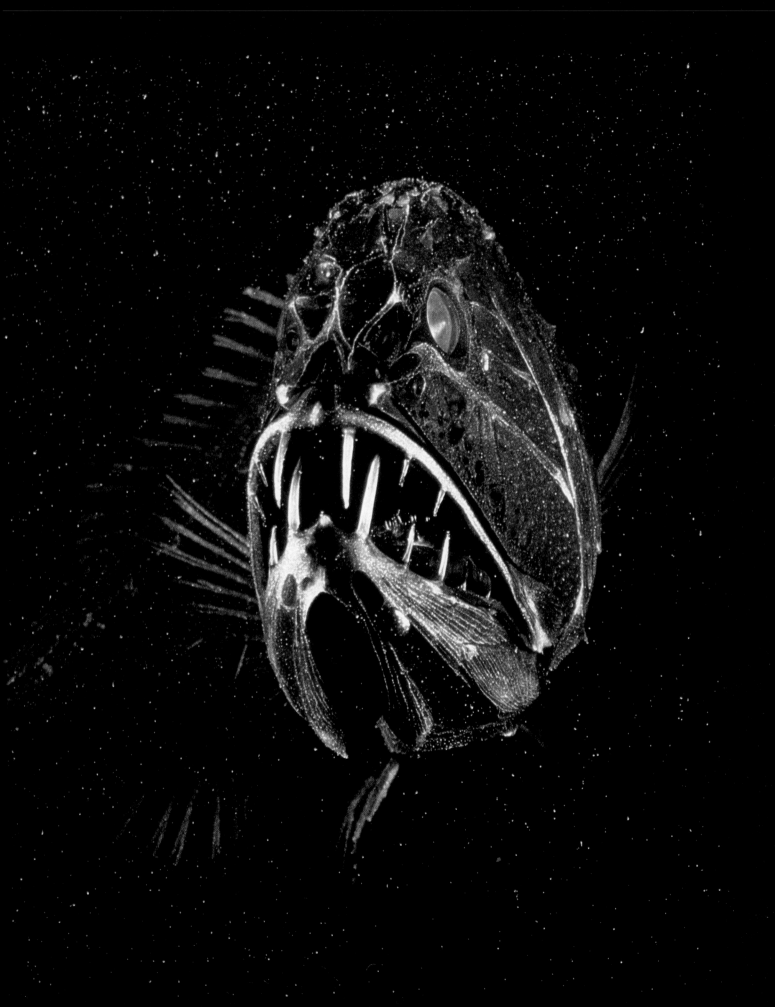

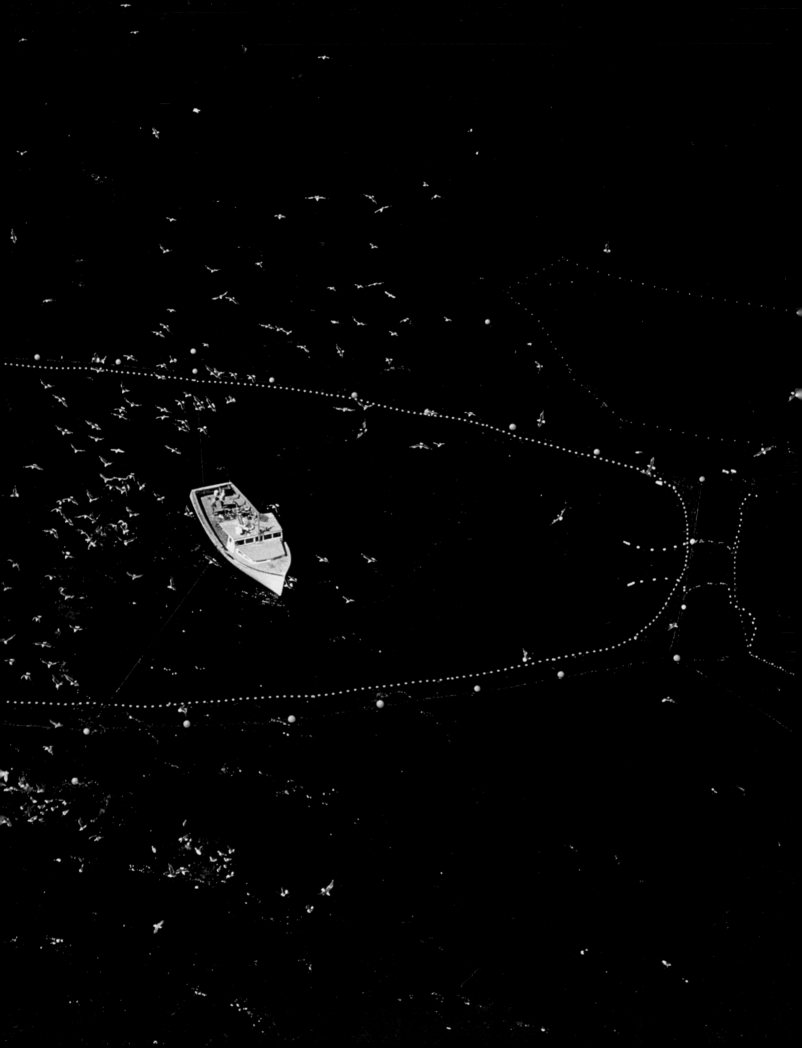

Chapter 5

THE STRUGGLE TO SAFEGUARD THE SEA

Carroll Livingston Riker had a grand dream. He envisioned nothing less than altering the climate of lands around the North Atlantic by shifting the course of an ocean current. A successful mechanical engineer who had helped plan the Panama Canal, Riker addressed his proposal to President Woodrow Wilson and to the United States Congress in 1913. His target was the Labrador Current, a flow of extremely cold Arctic water that runs along the coast of Canada to the tip of Newfoundland. There, the current turns eastward and, about 200 miles offshore in an area called the Grand Banks, intersects the Gulf Stream. Where the two meet, Riker wrote, the ice-cold current "delivers a refrigerating effect equivalent to the freezing of two million tons of ice every second onto the Bank and into the bosom of the warm north-flowing Gulf Stream." The stream, he added, "receives a staggering blow from which it never recovers." The blow not only chills the Gulf Stream but causes it to change course from northeast to southeast.

Riker reasoned that if the Gulf Stream were to continue on its original course its heat energy, which he estimated was "greater than that which could be released by the burning of one million tons of coal every minute," would raise temperatures in Greenland, the British Isles and Northern Europe by several degrees.

To shield the Gulf Stream from the Labrador Current, Riker proposed to divert the Arctic water with a 200-mile-long jetty extending from Newfoundland across the Grand Banks. Moreover, he would use the offending current itself to build the jetty. The Labrador Current carries with it great quantities of sand and gravel; Riker planned simply to put an obstacle in the path of the current along the sea bottom. The particles would pile up against this obstruction and form a sandbar, which would obstruct the flow even more and cause another layer of sand and gravel to accumulate. Gradually the bar would grow higher and higher until it reached the surface and completely blocked the current.

Riker saw benefits for the Grand Banks as well as for Europe. For one thing, the sandbar would bring relief from the dense fogs that were caused by the warm, humid air over the Gulf Stream being chilled by the Labrador Current; these fogs had long been the bane of both Grand Banks fishermen and transatlantic captains. And the most dangerous freight of the Labrador Current, the icebergs, would swirl away eastward out of the shipping lanes.

Riker's plan drew a mixed reaction. Many maritime organizations were enthusiastic, and *Scientific American* magazine offered to provide a team of

Accompanied by a flock of gulls, fish farmers tend bluefin tuna confined in a buoy-rimmed net cage off Nova Scotia. Of the approximately 72 million metric tons of fish harvested from the ocean every year, about five per cent are systematically raised or fattened at sites like this.

experts to assist in the planning of the project. On the other hand, there were many who were convinced the project would not work. And fishermen, despite the fog-free future envisioned by the plan, opposed the manipulation of the Labrador Current, which is laden with nutrients that make the waters of the Grand Banks a superlative place for marine life and, consequently, for commercial fishing.

Riker himself was sensitive to the international implications of his proposal, and he addressed it not only to the government of the United States but also to "officials of Interested Foreign Countries." He recognized that his plan might have calamitous results and suggested as a first step a study to assess the possible risks of tampering with the environment in such a godlike manner.

He was right to have been concerned. Later studies showed that while Northern Europe might have enjoyed a more temperate climate, so much of Greenland's icecap could have been melted by the altered Gulf Stream that heavily populated portions of the North Atlantic coastline might have been submerged. And as the skeptical fishermen thought, the diversion probably would have wreaked havoc with marine life and consequently with their livelihood.

At any rate, it seems to have been bad timing rather than perceived risk that defeated Riker's plan. Only a year after he had made his proposal, World War I erupted, and Congress declined to appropriate large sums for peacetime projects. By War's end, enthusiasm for Riker's grand jetty had diminished.

Whether it would have worked or not, Riker's plan was a harbinger of new attempts to exploit the food, energy and mineral resources of the sea in radically different ways, based on what oceanographers had learned about the complex dynamics of the oceans.

In the 100 years after the mid-19th Century, the world's total catch of fish — the ocean's most important product by far — increased roughly tenfold. Then the annual harvest tripled in just two decades, increasing from less than 20 million metric tons in 1948 to 64 million metric tons in 1969. In the next decade the catch continued to increase in volume — to 72 million metric tons in 1980 — but such statistics do not tell the whole story. Other profound changes had been taking place all

A National Marine Fisheries Service observer measures a fish taken by a Soviet trawler working in U.S. territorial waters. Besides monitoring size, observers make sure that foreign catches do not include lobsters, salmon or other high-profit marine species that are reserved solely for American fishermen.

along in the kinds of fish caught and in the size of regional catches.

For centuries, fishermen in the North Sea, where commercial fishing began, have pursued only a few of the estimated 20,000 species of finfish. These sought-after species, such as herring, cod and plaice, were once plentiful, but during the early part of the 20th Century, North Sea fishermen began to notice that their nets were bringing up smaller catches of smaller fish. It was apparent that the fish had been taken in such large quantities that they could no longer reproduce fast enough to maintain their former populations.

Attempts to conserve the supply were ineffectual because the fishermen of different countries could not agree on what limits they should place on their catches. Then World War I imposed a harsh remedy by halting most fishing. By the end of the War, the fish had had four years to mature and reproduce, and both catches and fish sizes were doubled. The supply gradually diminished again until World War II gave the fish another respite, during which their numbers increased by 400 per cent. In the years since World War II ended, the harvest of fish has dwindled once again.

The North Sea was not the only place where the catch of primary fish — those directly consumed by human beings — has decreased. In other parts of the North Atlantic, stocks of salmon, sturgeon and shad have become seriously depleted, as have sardines in the North Pacific. As the desirable primary fish became harder to find, fishermen began pursuing the Peruvian anchovy, the Atlantic menhaden and other so-called secondary fish, which because of their oiliness and pungent flavor are not widely used for direct human consumption. Most of the secondary catch is processed into meal and fed to livestock and poultry. Before World War II, 10 per cent of the world catch was converted to meal. In 1980, the share amounted to 30 per cent.

Marine biologists do not know how large a catch of primary fish species the oceans can sustain without irreversible damage, but many think it would be dangerous to push the annual harvest beyond 100 million metric tons. If more than that were taken, the remaining fish might not reproduce fast enough to maintain their populations. However, scientists readily admit that they are guessing. "The fact is," Canadian oceanographer L. M. Dickie has written, "that our knowledge of biological systems in the oceans is still a little like our knowledge of terrestrial biology a century ago, or of astronomy before Kepler."

Nevertheless, oceanographers who specialize in fisheries expect to help fishermen maintain their takes in ecologically sound ways. One major area of study is the life cycle of fish, their reproductive rates, patterns of migration and the relationship between different species inhabiting the same area. Little is known now, for instance, about what happens to other creatures in an ocean ecosystem when one species is heavily fished, but marine biologists assume that there are significant changes in population dynamics, competition for food and patterns of predation.

Scientists are also studying natural fluctuations in marine populations and their links to environmental changes, connections that are frequently misunderstood by the industries that depend on those populations. Maine lobstermen, for instance, were delighted by a 300 per cent increase in their catch during World War II. Many of them attributed their good fortune to the fact that Maine's offshore islands were practice targets for U.S. Navy bombers. The fishermen concluded that the bombing somehow disturbed the lobsters and made them easier to catch.

In fact, oceanographers have now come to believe that the increase in lobsters was caused by a warming trend that occurred in Maine waters. The temperature increased from 43.5° F. at the beginning of the War to 47° F. by War's end, and the latter reading is near the optimum for the growth and reproduction of lobsters. Yet while the lobstermen were bringing in fine catches, the fishermen who pursued cod and other cold-loving fish were suffering: As sea temperatures rose, these species migrated northward to more hospitable territory.

In the near future, scientists expect satellite observations to provide data that will be useful to fishermen. Color scanners on satellites, for example, can detect chlorophyll in ocean water. The primary pigment contained in phytoplankton, chlorophyll is an excellent index of biological activity; where it is abundant, fish are likely to gather. Satellites also collect data on sea-surface temperature, ice and cloud cover, and wind. In a pilot program in 1982, Japanese analysts used satellite data to predict likely locations for high concentrations of fish in the nation's territorial waters. Eighty per cent of the fishermen participating in the program reported that they found fish where the analysts had predicted they would be. Such schemes should eventually save fishing fleets much wasted time, effort and money.

A one-person research submersible called the *Wasp*, capable of descending to 2,000 feet, is lowered by cable from its mother ship. Foot-operated thrusters allow the scientist inside to control the *Wasp's* movement in order to collect interesting specimens with the clawlike manipulators. The infrared light mounted near the helmet, to the operator's left, is used to take photographs in the sunless depths.

Even when fishermen reach the supposed 100-million-ton limit in the worldwide annual take of primary fish, the ocean's ability to contribute protein to the human diet will be far from exhausted. Marine biologists estimate that 100 million tons of other marine creatures could safely be taken from the ocean each year without endangering future productivity. To take advantage of this underutilized marine bounty, fishermen and consumers will have to abandon habit and learn to value animals that occupy lower places in the ocean's food web.

The species that has received the most attention as a possible new food source for humans is krill, a shrimplike crustacean that averages about 2.5 inches in length. Huge rafts of krill occur in the high latitudes of the Southern Hemisphere. Before baleen whales were hunted almost to extinction, they used to converge by the hundreds of thousands on the fringes of the polar seas, gulping water and straining it through fringed bony plates in their mouths to extract the krill — up to three tons per day per whale. According to one calculation, the whales ate more than 250 million tons of krill annually, enough protein to sustain 200 million people for a year. One pound of krill yields more protein than an equal amount of finfish and supplies 460 calories and many essential vitamins.

The wholesale killing of whales has, from one point of view, freed a huge food supply that can be taken with little fear of ecological harm. And indeed ships from the U.S.S.R. and Japan have been trawling for krill in the Antarctic, which has the most bountiful supply, since the 1970s. The annual harvest, which reached 80,000 metric tons in 1979, is used partly for animal feed and partly for human food. But ecologists are concerned about the effects a greatly increased krill harvest would have on Antarctic creatures that feed on these crustaceans — penguins, seals, squid, fish, along with the few remaining baleen whales. The populations of the animals that once had to compete with whales for krill have burgeoned, but the appearance of a serious new competitor — the fisherman — could once again change the Antarctic's ecological balance and perhaps doom the baleen whales once and for all.

There are other marine creatures that supply humans with protein — squid and octopus, for instance. Certain European and Asian countries consume about a million and a half tons of these animals every year, and marine biologists estimate that the take could easily and safely be increased to seven million tons. The Japanese have never been particularly fond of sardines or mackerel, regarding these species as too bony and oily. But now processing machinery has been developed to reduce the oil content, and the Japanese are consuming great quantities of minced sardines and mackerel in a sausage called *surimi*. In the United States, minced fish finds its way into supermarkets in the guise of imitation scallops and crab legs.

Mariculture — the systematic farming of the open sea — offers still other possibilities for extracting food from the ocean. More closely allied to agriculture and animal husbandry than to traditional fishing, mariculture often begins with the transplanting of fish from one place to another.

Shortly after the turn of the century, British fisheries biologist Walter Garstang observed that the plaice, a popular commercial fish in the North Sea, regularly spawns in the Flemish Bight, located in the North Sea about midway between the coasts of Belgium and England. A current then pro-

A conveyor belt transports a catch of krill toward an automatic peeler on a Japanese factory ship in the Antarctic *(above)*. Shrimplike in appearance and flavor, the two-inch crustacean *(right)* is used in Japan as an ingredient in rice cakes, noodles and other processed foods.

pels the hatchlings to a feeding ground off the Dutch coast that, Garstang noted, often became so overcrowded with young plaice that the food supply could not support them all. Meanwhile the Dogger Bank, another feeding ground in the central North Sea between England and Denmark, harbored only a few plaice hatchlings. It was obviously hospitable to the species, since plaice old enough to swim on their own migrated there. Garstang caught thousands of young plaice in the spawning area in the Flemish Bight, measured them and tagged them. He then transported them in tanks of sea water to the Dogger Bank. After analyzing reports from the fishermen who caught tagged plaice, Garstang found that the transplanted plaice had grown at nearly three times the rate achieved by those caught along the overcrowded Dutch coast.

In a similar experiment, scientists in Denmark transplanted young plaice from overcrowded areas in the Baltic to the Lim Fjord, a Danish inland sea. The plaice grew so fast that the next fishing season in the Lim Fjord produced a harvest of plaice far larger than the year before and returned more than 10 times the cost of the transplanting. The Danish project, because it was carried out within the nation's borders, avoided a difficulty built into Garstang's experiment. The problem with transplanting fish to international waters such as the Dogger Bank was that no single country or association of trawler owners could be induced to pay for stocking waters where others could reap the results. Even though Europe's International Council for the Exploration of the Sea concluded in 1931 that transplanting would be profitable to all and recommended that it be continued, most of the council's member countries declined to comply.

In recent decades, however, several nations have transported hatchlings successfully halfway around the globe. Thanks to scientific analysis of potential new habitats and an increased understanding of the biological requirements of a particular species, some of these efforts have enjoyed considerable success.

One well-studied fish that has proved an adaptable emigrant is the Chinook salmon, which after being transplanted from its native waters off the Northwest Coast of the United States has become common off the shores of New Zealand. The salmon is a good choice for improving commercial stocks, since its annual appearance in certain parts of the ocean is highly predictable. After being spawned in fresh-water streams, young Chinook salmon migrate to the open ocean, where they live until they mature. Then they make their way back to their native streams to spawn. Each spring the homing fish appear in great "runs," which commercial fishermen can intercept offshore.

In 1980, biologists from the University of Washington transported fertilized Chinook eggs to southwestern Chile, where the coastal and marine environment is similar to that of the Pacific Northwest. The scientists released the eggs in streams that empty into the Pacific and awaited the results. Two years later, they were elated by reports that the first mature Chinooks had been spotted making their way up Chilean streams to spawn. Although they are uncertain where the fish spent their time in the ocean, biologists think it likely that the salmon will locate the plankton-rich feeding grounds in the region of the Antarctic Convergence, some 700 miles south of Chile. Here, nutrient-laden water flowing from the Antarctic meets and descends beneath the warmer waters of the Atlantic and the Pacific, creating ideal conditions for phytoplankton and, consequently, marine animals.

A more ambitious aim than stocking areas with new fish species is to alter an environment to make it more productive. Most of the world catch comes from the area of the continental shelves, which constitutes about 10 per cent of the ocean. The remaining 90 per cent is, in comparison, a biological desert, with scant marine life. Yet beneath these barren surfaces, sometimes no more than 300 feet down, lies water rich in phosphates and other nutrients. If this water could be brought to the surface, the desert might bloom with phytoplankton.

A number of schemes have been suggested — but not tested — for generating artificial upwelling. Columbus O'Donnel Iselin, a former director of the Woods Hole Oceanographic Institution, came up with the idea of anchoring large baffles near the sea bottom to divert the natural flow of cold bottom water upward. Iselin also suggested pumping air through a perforated hose laid along the bottom in shallow water; the escaping air bubbles would rise toward the surface and create an upwelling of water.

Oceanographers have examined other methods for boosting the productivity of ocean waters. Sir Alistair Hardy, a British zoologist, envisioned spreading phosphates to foster a higher phytoplankton growth rate. The principles of plant selection could be applied to marine species, just as they are to agricultural crops. For instance, strains of planktonic single-celled algae that have unusually high rates of photosynthesis could be dispersed in areas with good growing conditions to increase the food supply for zooplankton and fish.

Some scientists believe that the 80 to 100 million square miles of ocean that are now, from the human point of view, underproductive watery wastes have the potential to yield large quantities of fuel, food and other desirable products as full-fledged ocean farms. Howard A. Wilcox, an oceanographer with the U.S. Navy, has come up with a plan for an open-ocean farm whose principal crop would be the giant California kelp, a seaweed that grows in temperate coastal waters of both the eastern and western Pacific. In its natural habitat, kelp attaches itself to the sea bottom with structures called holdfasts. Buoyed by tiny air sacs, its shiny brown fronds grow upward to spread themselves across the surface, sometimes attaining lengths of 200 feet. Kelp beds on the California coast are harvested commercially and a substance called algin, which is used as a thickener, stabilizer or emulsifier in foods and industrial compounds, is extracted from the fronds.

On the deep-ocean kelp farm Wilcox envisions, a network of plastic lines submerged 40 to 100 feet deep and extending over as much as a square mile would provide the anchoring substratum for the kelp. A pump powered by wave or wind motion would raise cool subsurface water to fertilize the plants, whose fronds are capable of growing two feet per day. In the center of the farm would float a platform supporting buildings for farm workers and equipment.

Harvested and transported to the mainland for processing, the kelp crop would yield a number of useful products in addition to algin. Most important would be methane, a high-grade fuel that could be produced by fermenting the kelp. The residue of the fermentation process would retain enough carbohydrates and minerals to serve as a fertilizer for land crops or as animal feed.

The most promising locations for kelp farms are near the Equator, between lat. 15° S. and lat. 15° N., or in two bands girdling the earth in each of the temperate zones between lat. 25° and lat. 40°. These areas receive an

Fish ranchers toss mackerel and herring to their hungry stock of bluefin tuna from a workboat off the Nova Scotia coast. Bought in spring from local fishermen, the tuna are fattened in a net-enclosed open-ocean feed lot until October, when they are harvested and sold.

Five bluefin tuna that are part of an experimental breeding program are oblivious to a marine biologist who is inspecting their pen off the coast of

Sicily. Hormone treatments prompt the females to produce unusually large numbers of eggs.

abundance of sunshine to stimulate plant growth and are free of destructive hurricanes. Good light conditions, combined with the high fertility and cool temperature of the water pumped to the surface, might stimulate a burst of phytoplanktonic growth around the farm and a consequent increase in the fish population. Shellfish such as oysters could be grown in pens on the kelp farm.

With all its diversity, a deep-sea farm encompassing one square mile could produce enough food every year to feed 3,000 people. Wilcox estimates that oceanic food-energy farms eventually could support more than 20 billion people. A small, seven-acre pilot farm located 60 miles off the California coast was operated by the Navy under Wilcox's supervision in 1974 and 1975. That experience has convinced some oceanographers that kelp farms are technologically feasible, but their economic feasibility has yet to be demonstrated. Still, if traditional food and energy sources fail to meet the demands of a growing human population, kelp farms may become important supplements to land-based operations.

Scientists and engineers also are seeking a practical way to harness the boundless kinetic energy of the sea and convert it to human use. Water was the world's primary source of power from the invention of the water wheel 2,000 years ago until the 19th Century. Then it was displaced by the burning of wood, coal, oil and natural gas. Unlike all these fuels, and like the streams that once turned water wheels, waves seem to offer a source of energy whose use seems unlikely to have severe environmental consequences.

To put waves to work, U.S. engineer Demetrios Mountanos has devised an engagingly simple method. He was struck by the similarity between the movements of ocean waves and the motion of pistons in a reciprocating engine. "My attention," he explained, "has especially turned toward the ability of the waves to move any floating article up and down, including structures of thousands of tons. And when, in the summer of 1964, I conducted experiments on the coast of California, I saw that the waves produce powerful reciprocal strokes like those of diesel and steam engines."

Mountanos' experiment employed a chain-and-counterweight device for harnessing this rising and falling motion. Launching a heavy raft, he attached to it a chain that ran through a pulley in a fixed overhead crane and then ashore to a counterweight suspended from another pulley. As the raft rose and fell, the chain moved back and forth through the pulleys, and the counterweight ashore moved up and down. This regular motion activated a pump, which sent water into a reservoir to supply a hydroelectric plant. Mountanos calculated that the cost of the electricity generated by his wave-driven plant was far less than that of any conventional electric plant.

Sir Christopher Cockerell, the British inventor of the Hovercraft, has taken Mountanos' concept a step further by moving the pump out to sea aboard the raft. Cockerell's scheme uses the horizontal and vertical motions of the waves to power pumps on a series of rafts. The rafts are hinged together and aligned in the same direction that the waves are traveling. When the waves move under this string of rafts, one of them rises and moves forward while the one next to it moves backward and descends. A piston linked to the first raft moves back and forth in a cylinder on the adjoining raft. The piston-cylinder arrangement acts as a pump that moves sea water ashore to a hydroelectric station.

Another ingenious method for extracting energy from waves is called Salter's Duck after its inventor, engineer Stephen Salter of the University of Edinburgh. The apparatus consists of a large, round vane, 60 feet in diameter, that rises and falls with the waves. Anchored in water perhaps 300 feet deep, a line of these vanes would, by their reciprocating action, activate pumps to circulate oil through turbines to generate electricity.

A completely different method for extracting energy from ocean water is based on its thermal properties. The principle depends on the streams of cold water that slowly course their way through the depths of the sea. On both sides of the Equator, for about 100 miles, the temperature of the tropical surface water rarely falls below 80° F. The bottom water, which has come from the Arctic or Antarctic, is about 40° F. The difference between the two extremes is what could make thermal sea power possible.

An energy-producing system based on the transfer of heat in sea water was proposed as early as 1881, by French physicist Jacques d'Arsonval. But not until the 1930s was the idea given a practical test by one of d'Arsonval's students. Georges Claude had made a fortune with his invention of the neon light. He invested much of his money in thermal energy, first trying to tap the hot waste water from factories along the Meuse River in Belgium. Later, in the Caribbean off the coast of Cuba, he laid a long conduit on the bottom of the south slope of the Puerto Rico Trench to raise frigid water from the depths. Warm surface water was pumped into an evaporator — a chamber in which the atmospheric pressure was so drastically reduced that the water boiled at 80° F. (Ocean water boils at 212.1° F. when the atmospheric pressure is that of sea level.) The resulting steam turned a turbine to generate electricity, and then passed into a condensation chamber where it was quickly cooled and condensed by the cold bottom water. Claude's success attracted the attention of physicists and oceanographers, but his installation was destroyed by a hurricane. Claude did not rebuild it, and interest in thermal sea power languished until the early 1970s, when a differently engineered system, employing ammonia or freon to extract heat from sea water and drive turbines, was tried out by the U.S. government *(pages 102-103)*.

Thermal sea power could have some negative environmental effects. Meteorologists have raised questions about how the weather would react to the presence on the surface of huge amounts of cold water brought from the sea bottom. For one thing, the atmosphere around the plant would be cooled. For another, cold ocean water is saturated with carbon dioxide. As it warmed, the water would release much of this dissolved gas, and the balance of atmospheric gases could be disturbed. Marine biologists worry about the effect of thermal plants on local marine life. With more nutrients being brought to the surface by the cold water, both plant and animal species might burgeon, and local warm-water species might be displaced by others better adapted to cooler water. Such a phenomenon could, of course, be turned to advantage by fishermen.

In addition to forms of energy that may be tapped in the future, the ocean harbors a staggering supply of elements and minerals. A prime product is sodium chloride — close to half of world demand is met by salt extracted from ocean water. About 500 million tons of silver are dissolved in

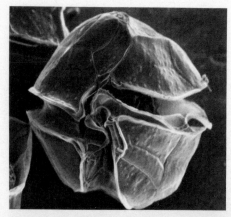

A noxious red tide blotches the ocean surface when certain brightly pigmented species of plankton multiply rapidly. The organisms (the one at left is shown 1,300 times life size in a scanning electron micrograph) produce a toxin that blocks nerve impulses and can kill humans.

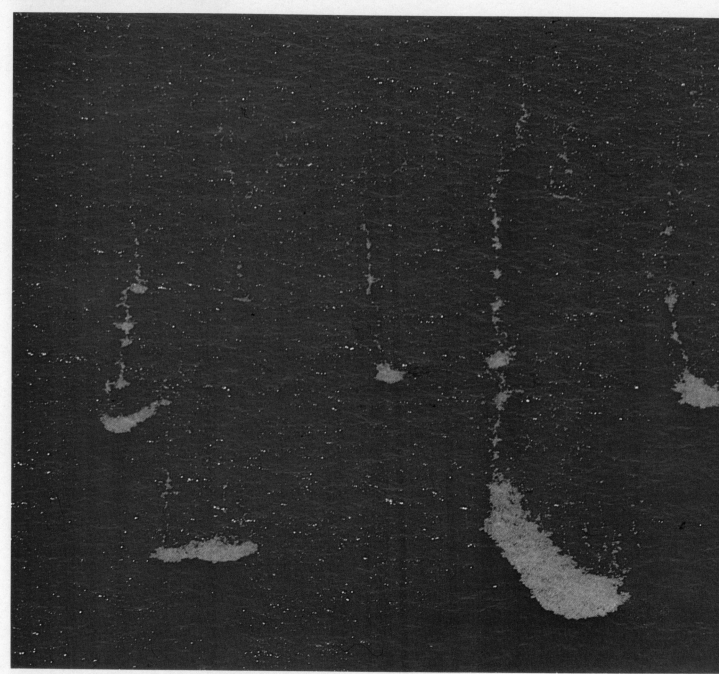

sea water, along with at least five billion tons each of uranium and copper. And there are perhaps 10 million tons of gold. But at present, filtering out any of these elements is uneconomical. Only two of the 84 elements known to exist in sea water are currently being extracted profitably: magnesium and bromine.

Not all the elements of the ocean are dispersed in water. Parts of the sea bottom are peppered with mineral-rich manganese nodules—spheres ranging in size from that of a pea to nearly 10 inches in diameter and composed principally of manganese, iron, nickel and copper. The material of the nodules precipitates out of sea water and forms in concentric rings around a nucleus, which may be a shark's tooth, a shell or a pebble. The nodules are found in very deep parts of the ocean, where the bottom is covered by only a very thin layer of sediment. Some manganese-nodule deposits, such as those in the North Pacific near Hawaii, are rich enough to make commercial exploitation likely, once the technology for dredging them up has been devised. But prospective miners will first have to resolve the question of ownership, since the nodules occur beneath international waters and belong to no one.

Ocean water does yield one highly valuable substance: fresh water. No fluid on earth is more abundant than sea water. And in many places near the ocean, the demand for fresh water far exceeds the supply, severely limiting agricultural and industrial growth. In the early 1980s, there were more than 1,500 plants around the world desalinating sea water and producing about 40 million gallons of fresh water daily. Economics, however, prevented the more widespread use of desalination, since the process was so expensive that in many arid areas it was cheaper to pipe water from sources hundreds of miles away. There were also environmental limitations, since treatment plants must be located in spots where ocean circulation is strong enough to sweep away the salty residue of the process. A build-up of briny wastes in an area of sluggish circulation can make it uninhabitable for indigenous plants, fish and other marine creatures.

For the thousands of years that people have fished and sailed the sea, the ocean has been a metaphor for something that changed yet always remained the same. But in the 20th Century the impact of industrial society on the ocean began to work enduring and unfortunate changes. For decade after decade wastes of all description had disappeared from sight under its waters. But while invisible to casual inspection, they were nevertheless having serious chemical, physical and biological effects on the ocean. It became increasingly apparent that using the ocean as a dump was not without peril. It also became apparent that society faced difficult environmental, economic and political decisions. Its toxic wastes had to be disposed of somewhere—on land or in the sea. Each choice entailed a price. DDT and other pesticides were washed downstream by rivers and spread through the sea by currents, at times in concentrations sufficient to poison its inhabitants. As the chemicals built up in the tissues of some species of sea birds, their eggshells thinned, causing a high rate of premature hatching. As a result, some species were endangered. DDT was found in the flesh of seals in the Arctic and penguins in the Antarctic. Industrial plants added to the highly varied and noxious flow—chlorides from foundries, sulfides from sugar refineries, cyanides from electroplating plants.

Oceanographers of the Woods Hole Oceanographic Institution found the Sargasso Sea littered with bits of plastic bobbing on the surface or floating just beneath it — the remains of bottles, clothespins, boxes, dishes and other plastic artifacts of a modern society. The flotsam and jetsam had followed the Atlantic currents in their slow circular swirl into the central Sargasso about 1,700 miles off the East Coast of the United States, where the oceanographers calculated that the refuse was concentrated as heavily as one piece per square yard of the surface. Many of these bits of plastic contained PCBs, highly toxic chemicals that have been shown to slow the growth rate of phytoplankton.

In 1982, twenty-five per cent of Americans lived in areas that had no sewage treatment systems at all, and many of the existing plants pumped partially treated sewage into rivers that transported it to the sea. Municipalities and states were dredging accumulated sediments from harbor and river bottoms to maintain channels or open new waterways and dumping the dredged material offshore. The U.S. Army Corps of Engineers has estimated that about 35 per cent of the dredgings are polluted by sewage or toxic heavy metals such as mercury.

In the United States, dredged material is dumped at offshore sites where the Environmental Protection Agency judges the risk of environmental damage to be minimal. Most of these sites are close to shore, but currents can transport some of the pollutants in the dredgings out into the open ocean. When sludge is disposed of in water whose temperature and density are fairly uniform from top to bottom, the particles fall quickly to the sea bottom. On the other hand, if there are layers of water present, with marked differences in temperature and density between adjoining layers, a horizontal flow could arise, deflect sludge particles from their downward path and transport them in unpredictable directions.

The sea has also been used as a dump site for obsolete military supplies, including shells, mines and other munitions. One method employed in the United States during the 1960s was to load surplus World War II Liberty ships with such items and scuttle them at sea; 19 of them, carrying more than 53,000 tons of scrap, were sunk during one seven-year period. Even such substances as rocket fuels and chemical weapons were tossed overboard to be carried away by the currents. The U.S. Army disposed of a large quantity of deadly nerve gas in the Florida Current. Though the gas was packed in containers designed to be impervious, the slightest leak could send the gas across the Atlantic via the Gulf Stream.

The fuel of the Industrial Age, oil, poses its own special threat to the oceans. As many as three million tons of oil enter the oceans every year from various sources. Huge spills from supertankers breaking up in storms or running aground receive dramatic publicity, but small-scale spills are a routine, chronic occurrence at offshore drilling rigs when tankers are taking on their cargo. Rivers and storm sewers also carry significant quantities of oil to the ocean. Residues of oil from automobile exhaust and smokestacks are blown out over the sea and drift down from the atmosphere to sink into ocean water. The Sargasso Sea is a catch basin for much of the Atlantic's oil pollution, along with solid wastes. During a cruise to study organisms of the Sargasso, Woods Hole oceanographers found the sargasso weed coated with oil. They had to suspend operations because of interference from tar balls — floating, asphalt-like agglomerations of oil that clogged their nets.

Wrote one of the scientists: "Some tows during this particular cruise netted more oil lumps than *Sargassum*."

In 1969 the sailor-explorer Thor Heyerdahl was astonished by the number of tar balls in the open ocean when he crossed the Atlantic in a small boat. During a 4,000-mile voyage across the equatorial Pacific aboard his raft *Kon-Tiki* in 1947, Heyerdahl had towed a fine-mesh plankton net and had scooped up no pollutants. Twenty-two years later, he found the Atlantic so clotted with "ugly clumps" of agglomerated petroleum that, he reported, "we were reluctant to dip up water with our buckets when we needed a good scrub-down at the end of the day." On a subsequent voyage Heyerdahl made an official survey for the United Nations, counting the tar balls and collecting some for laboratory examination. Their varying composition showed that they came from different shores of the Atlantic as well as from supertankers at sea.

Besides forming persistent tar balls, oil undergoes other physical and chemical processes in the ocean. Some of its heavier components settle to the bottom, while benzene, gasoline and other lighter components evaporate. There are also bacteria in the ocean that feed on oil, breaking it down into carbon dioxide and water.

Despite these various mechanisms, oil can leave long-lasting marks on the ocean. The best-studied tanker spill in history is that of the *Amoco Cadiz*, which went aground off Brittany in 1978 and lost 233,000 metric tons of oil. Oceanographers who have traced the fate of the *Amoco Cadiz* oil expect its residues, as well as the environmental changes it wrought along the Breton coast, to persist into the 1990s.

With the advent of the nuclear age at the end of World War II, governments had to decide on the safest, most practical and most economical methods for disposing of wastes containing man-made radioactive atoms, or radionuclides. Initially, the wastes resulted from the manufacture of atomic weapons, but the sources have multiplied over the years as more and more radionuclides are used in industry and medicine. Since a high dose of radioactivity or long-term exposure to low levels can cause cancer, genetic mutations and other severe health problems, all forms of radioactive wastes have demanded particularly careful and cautious handling.

As a repository for these radionuclides, the ocean appeared to offer several advantages over land sites. For one thing, it is a medium in which the radionuclides can be diluted and dispersed widely, perhaps to the point that they pose only a very small threat to human health. Even before the first atomic bomb was exploded in 1945, the dilute-and-disperse technique was used at a plant of the Columbia River in Washington, where plutonium was being produced for the first atomic bombs. River water that became radioactive after being used to cool the plutonium reactors ultimately reached the Pacific Ocean. Around the world, nuclear power plants and other industrial facilities routinely release their waste water — which contains lower levels of radioactivity than wastes of atomic-weapon manufacture — into rivers and estuaries that transport it to the open sea.

At the same time, the ocean offers greater isolation for wastes than is possible at most land sites; radioactive wastes can be dumped hundreds of miles from shore and sunk to depths of thousands of feet. Many governments, including those of the United States, Great Britain, Switzerland and France, decided in the postwar years that ocean dumping posed a smaller risk to human beings than land disposal. These wastes were sealed in concrete-and-steel drums and dropped in waters 13,000 feet or more deep. By 1982, more than 90,000 metric tons of radioactive wastes had been deposited in the northeast Atlantic alone.

Deep-ocean studies had located bottom areas where the water is virtually stagnant and probably would not carry radioactivity far from a container even if a leak should occur. But many marine scientists were concerned about safety. They thought that too little was known about such things as upwelling and convection currents, which might transport radionuclides to the surface. Another worry was that these radionuclides might enter the food web. In the sunless depths of the ocean dumps, of course, there are no plankton and very few fish. But radionuclides brought to the surface would come in contact with plants and animals. The fear was not without basis: After an atomic bomb test at Bikini atoll in 1954, plankton absorbed radioactivity and passed it on to predators, including tuna that were caught far from the testing site.

In the United States, opposition to ocean dumping increased during the 1960s and in 1972 culminated in the Marine Protection Research and Sanctuaries Act. The Act banned ocean dumping of high-level radioactive wastes altogether and put such severe restrictions on less toxic solid wastes that no permits were issued for ocean disposal during the next decade. Instead, these wastes were all held in storage facilities scattered around the nation.

But the issue of dumping high-level wastes is not a dead one. In 1982 ecologists were alarmed when the U.S. Navy announced a long-term plan to scuttle as many as 100 decommissioned nuclear submarines off the East and West Coasts of the United States. The subs would of course be defueled. Even a working nuclear submarine, if sunk by accident, may present little or no danger: When the U.S. submarine *Thresher* sank off Nova Scotia in 1963, Admiral Hyman Rickover quickly issued a statement: "I can assure you there is no radioactive hazard as a result of this unfortunate accident. Reactors of the type used in the *Thresher*, as well as in all our nuclear submarines and surface ships, can remain submerged indefinitely in sea water without creating any hazard." In the case of the *Thresher*, no radioactive contamination was found near the site where the sub disappeared. Still, experts not so committed to a nuclear navy as Admiral Rickover maintained that even without their fuel, these obsolete nuclear submarines were far from being free of radioactivity. One ecological organization, the Oceanic Society, claimed that the radioactivity still lingering in each of these defueled vessels could be one and a half times as great as the total radioactivity known to have been disposed of in American waters since ocean dumping began in 1946.

Nor did the two proposed disposal sites appeal to critics of the Navy's plan: One lay 160 miles southwest of Cape Mendocino, California, under the strong California Current, and the other 220 miles southeast of Cape Hatteras, North Carolina, at a spot known as the Graveyard of the Atlantic because of the strong local currents and storms that have caused thousands of shipwrecks. The Gulf Stream passes through this area, and a deep countercurrent runs beneath it.

Many of the countries that have continued to dispose of radioactive wastes in the oceans have followed the practices recommended by the Inter-

A ship discharges sludge from a sewage-treatment plant into 100-foot-deep waters off Long Island, New York. After years of such dumping, layers of sludge as thick as 35 feet have accumulated at some sites in the shallow waters along the U.S. East Coast.

An assortment of trash mixed with leaves and pieces of wood moves slowly seaward off the coast of Borneo. Unlike organic matter, which decays readily in sea water, plastic items can persist for years and travel thousands of miles in the ocean currents.

national Atomic Energy Agency. This United Nations agency has urged countries to use the "critical pathway" method of evaluating the risk posed by a dumping program. A critical pathway is the means by which radionuclides in ocean water could reach the general public or a particular group of people — oyster fishermen, beachcombers or bait diggers, for example — in dangerous quantity.

Determining a critical pathway can involve painstaking detective work and on occasion lead to a surprise. One such case occurred in Britain in the 1970s. The site was the Windscale plutonium plant on the Irish Sea in Cumberland, England. Windscale disposes of its own spent fuel and that of other British nuclear facilities. The currents near Windscale form a backwater, so that the waste water from the plant tends to move back and forth off the local coast, diffusing gradually into the northern and southern currents of the Irish Sea, by which time its radioactivity has been diluted, supposedly well below dangerous concentrations.

When physicist H. J. Dunster was assigned to make sure that the disposal method was safe, he studied the area along the Cumberland coast. His tests showed that the beaches were safe for swimming and that the only

A noose of plastic line discarded in the South Atlantic now painfully constricts the muscular neck of a fur seal on South Georgia Island. Young seals often playfully slip their heads through such circular objects, which can cause severe injury or death as the animals grow.

radioactivity absorbed by fish was concentrated in their intestines, which are removed when the fish are cleaned for eating. The only possible source of danger, Dunster found, was *Porphyra umbilicalis,* a local seaweed called the purple laver, which collects an inordinate amount of radioactivity in its lettuce-like leaves. Dunster also discovered that Englishmen along the coast near Windscale harvest this seaweed and ship it to South Wales, where it is eaten raw or cooked in a mash called laver bread.

If the seaweed is consumed in small quantities — and it is generally used as a condiment — the contamination is not enough to endanger anyone's health. But Dunster persisted in his investigation and found two Welshmen who ate more than a pound of it per day. Dunster took care of this problem simply by making sure that the radioactive level of the water released into the Irish Sea at Windscale was low enough that anyone could eat a couple of pounds of *Porphyra umbilicalis* a day. The case of the two unsuspecting Welshmen underscores the constant and careful monitoring required to minimize the risk of unwitting and possibly lethal overdoses of radiation.

Rachel Carson was one of the first to warn of the spread of pollution by ocean currents. In 1960 she wrote that "all recent knowledge points to far greater activity at all levels of the sea than had ever been guessed at. The deep turbulence, the horizontal movements of vast rivers of ocean water streaming one above another in varying directions, the upwelling of the water from the depths carrying with it minerals from the bottom, and the opposite downward sinking of great masses of surface water, all result in a gigantic mixing process that in time will bring about universal distribution of the radioactive contaminants."

A decade later, ecologists from 30 nations gathered on the island of Malta for a convocation called Pacem in Maribus — Peace in the Oceans — to discuss what was happening to the seas of the world. Pointing to highly polluted portions of the Mediterranean around them as an example of what could happen to the larger oceans in time, British scientist Lord Peter Ritchie-Calder predicted, "Things will get worse because effects will be multiplied by the increase in industrial activity without adequate services to deal with the wastes. The health of millions will be in danger." The official proclamation of Pacem in Maribus was even stronger. "The time has come to face the terrible fact that our oceans and the seas are threatened with destruction."

Yet 10 years after the Pacem in Maribus convocation, U.S. oceanographer George Harvey concluded a study of the oceans by the United Nations Regional Seas Program by announcing: "We all feel that the ocean is healthier in 1982 than it was in 1972." One major reason for the seas' improved bill of health was the growing environmental awareness of the 1960s and, consequently, the practical steps taken in the 1970s to lower the level of ocean pollution. Tighter laws in most industrial countries reduced the discharge of petroleum and other pollutants and placed new restrictions on the use of pesticides, which are borne to the sea in rivers.

One important contribution to the cleanup was an international agreement reached in 1973 to limit the disposal of tanker washings at sea. Before then, a ship's empty oil tanks were washed out with sea water, and the oily wash water was discharged directly into the ocean. The new cleaning method, called "load on top," involves pumping a ship's wash water into one of its tanks. When the oil rises to the top, the water beneath it is jettisoned, and the residue is kept aboard. At the oil terminal the new cargo of crude is loaded on top of it, and when the tanker unloads at the refinery, the residue is removed and disposed of there, thus keeping it out of the ocean.

Pollution control has not been the only reason for the oceans' improving health. The natural ability of the sea to cleanse itself is probably a greater factor than any human regulations. The most striking conclusion that was reached by the 100 scientists from three dozen countries who participated in the United Nations study was, as George Harvey put it, that "the ocean is more resilient and able to protect itself than we had thought."

The oceanographers, marine biologists and other scientists who took part in the four-year examination were not surprised to find numerous coastal areas still polluted by petroleum, sewage and industrial effluents. But the largest share of these pollutants were dispersed in a sea that — so far — has been able to assimilate them. The findings of the United Nations study were echoed by Woods Hole oceanographer Derek Spencer, who agreed that "the ocean has some important self-cleaning processes that we didn't know about until recently."

Yet the contamination of coastal areas and such gyral centers as the Sargasso Sea are cited by oceanographers who are concerned about the long-range effects of continuing pollution of the sea. They point out that many mysteries remain. Are all bottom currents as slow as those measured so far? Will currents concentrate pollutants in the centers of gyres? What still-unguessed oceanic processes might occur? What unpredictable product might result from pollutants mixing in the ocean?

And what about the food web? Will tolerable levels of heavy metals in the water become concentrated into lethal levels as they pass upward through this web? Will the effects be spread by migratory fish? And could the carbon dioxide that is spewed into the air by burning fossil fuels and absorbed by the oceans disrupt the chemical balance of sea water? Some scientists have even conjectured that an excess of carbon dioxide could slow the vertical gyres of the ocean and disrupt its circulation.

Despite remarkable advances, oceanography is poised at a new frontier that is as bewildering and challenging as it is promising. Even though far better informed than the scientists of just a few decades ago, today's oceanographer still does not know enough of the oceans to predict confidently all the effects of human activity on them. As one marine biologist put it, "We don't even know what to predict in a natural environment, much less a polluted one." But it has become evident that any pronounced change introduced into the ocean by human activity could burden future generations with dangerous and irreversible environmental damage. As biologist and lawyer Kenneth S. Kamlet of the National Wildlife Federation has observed, "If it turns out we are being more protective than necessary, posterity will forgive us." **Ω**

A majestic humpback whale erupts from the Pacific Ocean near Hawaii. Once endangered by unchecked hunting, the species has become a symbol of

human depredation; yet it also represents the growing hope for an improved ocean ecosystem through international controls.

ACKNOWLEDGMENTS

The editors thank: *In Finland:* Helsinki — Institute of Marine Research; Hannu Grönvall, Dr. Kimo Kahma, Dr. Pentti Malkki, Dr. Lauri Niemistö, Institute of Marine Research; Professor Aarno Voipio, Baltic Marine Environment Protection Commission. *In France:* Brest Naval — Capitaine de Vaisseau Michel Voirin, Ceppol; Lannion — Michèle Champagne, Centre de Météorologie Spatiale; Marseilles — Hans-Joachim Minas, Laboratoire d'Océanographie, Faculté des Sciences; Nantes — Gilbert Damy, C.O.B.; Paris — Claude Benoit, Secrétariat d'État à la Mer; Michel Crépon, Laboratoire d'Océanographie Physique, Museum National d'Histoire Naturelle; François Doumenge, Museum National d'Histoire Naturelle; Lucien Laubier, Philippe Marchand, François Vitali-Jacob, Press Attaché, C.N.E.X.O.; Toulouse — Michel Lefebvre, C.N.E.S.; Villefranche-Sur-Mer — André Morel, Laboratoire de Physique et de Chimie Marine. *In Great Britain:* Aberdeen — H. D. Dooley, Marine Laboratory, Department of Agriculture and Fisheries for Scotland; Cambridge — Anne Todd, British Antarctic Survey; Coventry — Dr. Norman Bellamy, Brian Loughridge, Dr. P.R.S. White, Wave Energy Project, Coventry Polytechnic; Edinburgh — David Jeffrey, Dr. S. H. Salter, Jamie Taylor, Department of Mechanical Engineering, Edinburgh University; Harwell (Oxon) — Deirdre Edwards, Energy Technology Support Unit; London — Gordon Hanlon, Dr. Anita McConnell, Science Museum; Lowestoft (Suffolk) — Robert Dickson, Fisheries Laboratory, Ministry of Agriculture, Fisheries and Food; Redhill (Surrey) — Richard White, Editor, International Power Generation; Southampton — Margaret Deacon Seward, Oceanography Department, University of Southampton; Wormley (Surrey) — Dr. Martin Angel, Sir George Deacon, Laurie Draper, Peter Herring, Arnold Madgwick, Denise Smythe Wright, Roy Wild, Institute of Oceanographic Sciences. *In Italy:* Naples — Sebastiano Genovese, Donato Marino, Stazione Zoologica; Arturo de Maio, Istituto Universitario Navale; Rome — John Gulland, Fish Stock Evaluation Branch, Food and Agriculture Organization of the United Nations; Pier Domenico Petrelli, Progetto Finalizzato Oceanografia e Fondi Marini, CNR; Capt. Salvatore Scotto di Santillo, Armamento Navi Oceanografiche,

CNR. *In Japan:* Shimizu — Dr. Yuzo Komaki, Far Seas Fisheries Research Laboratory; Tokyo — Dr. Hisashi Kanno, Dr. Satoshi Mito, Japan Fisheries Agency; Hiroshi Kasai, Akihiko Ueda, Japan Science and Technology Agency; Dr. Hideo Nitani, Tadao Tatsuno, Maritime Safety Agency; Masanori Takahashi, Japan Marine Fishery Resource Research Center; Professor Takahisa Nemoto, Professor Toshihiko Nemoto, University of Tokyo. *In Monaco:* Christian Carpine, Curator, Musée Océanographique. *In the Netherlands:* The Hague — Koninklijke Marine (The Royal Dutch Navy); Rijkswatersstaat; Hilversum — Martin de Vries; Texel — N.I.O.Z. (Dutch Institute for Research of the Seas); C. Veth. *In New Zealand:* Auckland — Dr. R. V. Grace; Christchurch — Dr. K. Westerskov; Nelson — G. R. Roberts; Ngunguru — Wade Doak; Otago — Dr. J. B. Jillet, Director, Dr. J. Zeldis, Portobello Marine Laboratory, University of Otago; Upper Hutt — Brian Enting; Wellington — Dr. K. Grange; Dr. D. E. Hurley, Director, New Zealand Oceanographic Institute. *In the United States:* California — (Corono del Mar) Dr. Wheeler North, Kerchoff Marine Laboratory, California Institute of Technology; (La Jolla) Craig Cary, Bear Flag Films; Professor Joseph L. Reid, Scripps Institution of Oceanography; Scripps Institution of Oceanography; (Pasadena) Kevin Hussey, Jet Propulsion Laboratory; (Santa Barbara) Bruce Robison, University of California; District of Columbia — Dr. Robert Gibbs, Department of Vertebrate Zoology, Smithsonian National Museum of Natural History; Jan K. Herman, Naval Medical Command; Raymond Hagan, Dick James, Office of the Oceanographer of the Navy, U.S. Naval Observatory; Florida — (Miami) Dr. Otis Brown, University of Miami; Maryland — (Germantown) Dr. William O. Forster, Dr. Charles L. Osterberg, Ecological Research Division, U.S. Department of Energy; (Mt. Airy) Dr. William Conner, National Marine Pollution Program Office, National Oceanographic and Atmospheric Adminstration (NOAA); (Rockville) Dr. Glenn Flittner, National Ocean Service; Betty Littlejohn, NOAA; (Upper Marlboro) Vilhelm Bjerknes, Climate Analysis Center, National Weather Service; Massachusetts — (Cambridge) Dr. A. R. Robinson, Harvard University; Professor Carl

Wunsch, Massachusetts Institute of Technology; (Marion) John Brokow, Christopher A. Sampson, Sippican Ocean Systems, Inc.; (Woods Hole) Nancy Green, Dr. Charles Hollister, Dean of Graduate Studies, Terrence Joyce, Department of Physical Oceanography, Dr. Philip L. Richardson, Associate Scientist, Henry M. Stommel, Senior Scientist, Peter Wiebe, Department of Physical Oceanography, Dr. John Whitehead, Woods Hole Oceanographic Institution; New York — (New York) Jean E. Parvin, Basic Resources Corporation; Oregon — (Corvallis) Dudley Chelton, School of Oceanography, Oregon State University; Texas — (College Station) Terry Anderson, Oral History Collection, Texas A & M University; Virginia — (Arlington) Michael J. McKisic, Office of Naval Research; Washington — (Seattle) Dr. Murray Hayes, National Marine Fisheries Service, NOAA. *In West Germany:* Bonn — Helmut Schulz, Bundesministerium für Forschung und Technologie; Bremerhaven — Hans-Peter Marschall, Alfred-Wegener-Institut für Polarforschung; Hamburg — Günter Heise, Deutsches Hydrographisches Institut; Dr. Friedrich Krügler; Susanne Schapowalow; Dr. Hjalmar Thiel, Institut für Hydrobiologie und Fischereiwissenschaft, Universität Hamburg; Kiel — Dr. Uwe Kils, Dr. Johannes Kinzer, Dr. John Woods, Institut für Meereskunde, Universität Kiel.

Useful sources of information and quotations for this volume were: *The World Ocean: An Introduction to Oceanography* by William A. Anikouchine and Richard W. Sternberg, Prentice-Hall, 1981; *The Oceans* by Robert Barton, London, Aldus Books, 1980; *Oceanography: A View of the Earth* by M. Grant Gross, Prentice-Hall, 1982; *Ocean World Encyclopedia* by Donald G. Groves and Lee M. Hunt, McGraw-Hill, 1980; *Exploring the Ocean World: A History of Oceanography,* edited by C. P. Idyll, Crowell, 1969; *Oceanography: Contemporary Readings in Ocean Sciences* by R. Gordon Pirie, Oxford University Press, 1977; *Rand McNally Atlas of the Oceans,* Rand McNally, 1977; *Introduction to Oceanography* by David A. Ross, Prentice-Hall, 1982; *The Edge of an Unfamiliar World: A History of Oceanography* by Susan Schlee, E. P. Dutton, 1973; *Introductory Oceanography* by Harold V. Thurman, Charles E. Merrill, 1981. The index was prepared by Gisela S. Knight.

BIBLIOGRAPHY

Books

Angel, Martin and Heather, *Ocean Life*. London: Octopus Books, 1974.

Anikouchine, William A., and Richard W. Sternberg, *The World Ocean: An Introduction to Oceanography*. Prentice-Hall, 1981.

Bartlett, Jonathan, ed., *The Ocean Environment*. H. W. Wilson, 1977.

Barton, Robert, *The Oceans*. London: Aldus Books, 1980.

Brewer, Peter G., ed., *Oceanography: The Present and Future*. Springer-Verlag, 1983.

Carson, Rachel L., *The Sea around Us*. Oxford University Press, 1961.

Dampier, William, *A New Voyage round the World*. Dover, 1968.

Deacon, G.E.R., ed., *Oceans: An Atlas History of Man's Exploration of the Deep*. London: Paul Hamlyn, 1962.

Deacon, G.E.R. and Margaret B., eds., *Modern Concepts of Oceanography*. Hutchinson Ross, 1982.

Deacon, Margaret, *Scientists and the Sea, 1650-1900: A Study of Marine Science*. Academic Press, 1971.

Deacon, Margaret B., ed., *Oceanography: Concepts and History*. Dowden, Hutchinson & Ross, 1978.

Delpar, Helen, ed., *The Discoverers: An Encyclopedia of Explorers and Exploration*. McGraw-Hill, 1980.

Earle, Sylvia A., and Al Giddings, *Exploring the Deep Frontier: The Adventure of Man in the Sea*. National Geographic Society, 1980.

Gaskell, T. F., *The Gulf Stream*. John Day, 1972.

Gordon, Bernard L., *Man and the Sea: Classic Accounts of Marine Explorations*. Book & Tackle Shop, 1980.

Gross, M. Grant:
Oceanography, 4th ed., Charles E. Merrill, 1980.
Oceanography: A View of the Earth, 3rd ed. Prentice-Hall, 1982.

Groves, Donald G., and Lee M. Hunt, *Ocean World Encyclopedia*. McGraw-Hill, 1980.

Guberlet, Muriel L., *Explorers of the Sea: Famous Oceanographic Expeditions*. Ronald Press, 1966.

Haines, Gregory, *Sound Underwater*. Crane Russak, 1974.

Hardy, Sir Alister, *The Open Sea: Its Natural History*, Parts 1 and 2. Houghton Mifflin, 1970.

Harvey, John G., *Atmosphere and Ocean: Our Fluid Environments*. Artemis Press, 1976.

Hickling, C. F., and Peter Lancaster Brown, *The Seas and Oceans in Color*. Macmillan, 1973.

Hollaender, Alexander, ed., *The Biosaline Concept: An Approach to the Utilization of Underexploited Resources*. Plenum Press, 1982.

Idyll, C. P., *Abyss: The Deep Sea and the Creatures That Live in It*. Crowell, 1976.

Idyll, C. P., ed., *Exploring the Ocean World: A History of Oceanography*. Crowell, 1969.

Intergovernmental Oceanographic Commission, *The International Decade of Ocean Exploration (IDOE), 1971-1980*. UNESCO, 1974.

Jensen, Albert C., *Wildlife of the Oceans*. Harry N. Abrams, 1979.

Linklater, Eric, *The Voyage of the Challenger*. London: Sphere Books, 1974.

McConnell, Anita, *No Sea Too Deep: The History of Oceanographic Instruments*. Bristol, England: Adam Hilger, 1982.

Maury, Matthew Fontaine, *The Physical Geography of the Sea and Its Meteorology*. Belknap Press, 1963.

Menard, H. W., ed., *Ocean Science: Readings from Scientific American*. W. H. Freeman, 1977.

Moore, J. Robert, *Oceanography: Readings from Scientific American*. W. H. Freeman, 1971.

Mountfield, David, *A History of Polar Exploration*. Dial Press, 1974.

Murray, John, *Selections from Report on the Scientific Results of the Voyage of H.M.S. Challenger during the Years 1872-76*. Arno Press, 1977.

Nansen, Dr. Fridtjof, *Farthest North*, Vols. 1 and 2. Harper, 1902.

National Geographic Society, *The Ocean Realm.* National Geographic Society, 1978.

Newberry, Andrew Todd, *Life in the Sea: Readings from Scientific American.* W. H. Freeman, 1982.

Parks, Peter, *Underwater Life: The World You Never See.* Hamlyn, 1976.

Perry, A. H., and J. M. Walker, *The Ocean-Atmosphere System.* Longman, 1977.

Pickard, George L., and William J. Emery, *Descriptive Physical Oceanography: An Introduction.* Pergamon Press, 1982.

Pirie, R. Gordon, ed., *Oceanography: Contemporary Readings in Ocean Sciences.* Oxford University Press, 1977.

Polmar, Norman, *Death of the Thresher.* Chilton Books, 1964.

Raitt, Helen, and Beatrice Moulton, *Scripps Institution of Oceanography: First Fifty Years.* Ward Ritchie Press, 1967.

Rand McNally Atlas of the Oceans. Rand McNally, 1977.

Reader's Digest, *Secrets of the Seas: Marvels and Mysteries of Oceans and Islands.* Reader's Digest, 1972.

Riker, Carroll Livingston, *Power and Control of the Gulf Stream.* Scientific Press, 1912.

Robinson, A. R., ed., *Eddies in Marine Science.* Springer-Verlag, 1983.

Ross, David A., *Introduction to Oceanography.* 3rd ed. Prentice-Hall, 1982.

Schlee, Susan:
The Edge of an Unfamiliar World: A History of Oceanography. E. P. Dutton, 1973.
On Almost Any Wind: The Saga of the Oceanographic Research Vessel Atlantis. Cornell University Press, 1978.

Scientific American, *The Ocean.* W. H. Freeman, 1969.

Sears, M., and D. Merriman, eds., *Oceanography: The Past.* Springer-Verlag, 1980.

Shor, Elizabeth Noble, *Scripps Institution of Oceanography: Probing the Oceans, 1936-1976.* Tofua Press, 1978.

Skinner, Brian J., and Karl K. Turekian, *Man and the Ocean.* Prentice-Hall, 1973.

Smith, F. G. Walton, *The Seas in Motion.* Crowell, 1973.

Stommel, Henry, *The Gulf Stream: A Physical and Dynamical Description.* 2nd ed. University of California Press, 1976.

Taber, Robert W., and Harold W. Dubach, *1001 Questions Answered about the Oceans and Oceanography.* Dodd, Mead, 1972.

Teal, John and Mildred, *The Sargasso Sea.* Little, Brown, 1975.

Thomson, Sir C. Wyville, *The Atlantic: The Voyage of the "Challenger,"* Vol. 1. Harper & Brothers, 1878.

Thorndike, Joseph J., Jr., ed., *Mysteries of the Deep.* American Heritage, 1980.

Thurman, Harold V., *Introductory Oceanography.* 3rd ed. Charles E. Merrill, 1981.

Turekian, Karl K., *Oceans.* Prentice-Hall, 1976.

Vetter, Richard C., ed., *Oceanography: The Last Frontier.* Basic Books, 1973.

Vogt, Per, et al., *Fridtjof Nansen: Explorer, Scientist, Humanitarian.* Oslo: Dreyers Forlag, 1961.

Voss, Gilbert L., *Oceanography.* Golden Press, 1972.

Ward, Ritchie, *Into the Ocean World: The Biology of the Sea.* Alfred A. Knopf, 1974.

Warren, Bruce A., and Carl Wunsch, eds., *Evolution of Physical Oceanography: Scientific Surveys in Honor of Henry Stommel.* MIT Press, 1981.

Williams, Jerome, John J. Higginson and John D. Rohrbough, *Sea & Air: The Marine Environment.* Naval Institute Press, 1973.

Wüst, Georg, *The Stratosphere of the Atlantic Ocean: Scientific Results of the German Atlantic Expedition of the Research Vessel "Meteor" 1925-27,* Vol. 6, Section 1. Ed. and transl. by William J. Emery. New Delhi: Amerind Publishing, 1978.

Periodicals

Branning, Timothy G., "Giant Kelp: Its Comeback against Urchins, Sewage." *Smithsonian,* September 1976.

Butler, James N., "Pink Stripe on the Ocean." *Natural History,* July 1980.

Butler, Michael J. A., "Plight of the Bluefin Tuna." *National Geographic,* August 1982.

"Can the Sea Purge Itself?" *Newsweek,* August 31, 1981.

Charlier, Roger H., "Ocean-Fired Power Plants." *Sea Frontiers,* January/February 1981.

Chelton, Dudley B., Kevin J. Hussey and Michael E. Parke, "Global Satellite Measurements of Water Vapour, Wind Speed and Wave Height." *Nature,* December 10-16, 1981.

Daly, Kathy, "Mid-Ocean Dynamics Experiment (MODE)." *Naval Research Reviews,* April 1976.

"Detente of the High Seas." *Life,* August 1983.

Donaldson, Lauren R., and Timothy Joyner, "The Salmonid Fishes as a Natural Livestock." *Scientific American,* July 1983.

"Drought, Death and Despair." *Time,* July 11, 1983.

Earle, Sylvia A., "Undersea World of a Kelp Forest." *National Geographic,* September 1980.

Fine, John C., "River in the Ocean." *The Lamp,* Summer 1978.

"Flood, Typhoon, Tornado — and Drought." *Discover,* June 1983.

Frisch, Joan Vandiver, "Sailing Ships and Satellites Explore the Secrets of Waves beneath the Sea." *NOAA Magazine,* April 1975.

Golden, Frederic, "Tracking That Crazy Weather." *Time,* April 11, 1983.

Gregg, Michael C., "The Microstructure of the Ocean." *Scientific American,* February 1973.

Griffin, Owen M., "Power from the Oceans' Thermal Gradients." *Sea Technology,* August 1977.

Hilts, Philip J., "El Niño Weather Disasters Continue." *The Washington Post,* June 14, 1983.

Hoyle, Russ, "Australia's 'Great Day.'" *Time,* March 28, 1983.

Kerr, Richard A.:
"Acoustic Tomography of the Ocean." *Science,* July 2, 1982.
"Fingers of Salt Help Mix the Sea." *Science,* January 9, 1981.

Loftas, Tony, "Pollution Peril Pervades Ocean." *The Christian Science Monitor,* July 13, 1971.

Marden, Luis, "The Continental Shelf: Man's New Frontier." *National Geographic,* April 1978.

Matthews, Samuel W.:
"New World of the Ocean." *National Geographic,* December 1981.
"Science Explores the Monsoon Sea." *National Geographic,* October 1967.

Murphy, Robert Cushman, "Among the Pearl Islands." *Natural History,* June 1944.

"Ocean Circulation: A Stirring Tale." *Mosaic,* September/October 1979.

Oceans, January 1968-May/June 1983.

Oceanus, Winter 1952-Summer 1983.

Olson, Steve, "The Contours Below." *Science 83,* July/August 1983.

Osterberg, Charles L., "The Ocean: Nature's Trash Basket." *Waste Management '82,* March 8-11, 1982.

Rasmusson, Eugene M., and J. Michael Hall, "The Major Pacific Warm Episode of 1982/83." *World Meteorological Organization Bulletin,* October 1983.

Rensberger, Boyce, "Plastic Is Found in Sargasso Sea." *The New York Times,* March 19, 1972.

Ricciuti, Edward R., "Farms Beneath the Waves." *Geo,* May 1981.

Richardson, P. L.:
"Progress on the Gulf Stream." *Geographical,* May 1980.
"Walter Hoxton's 1735 Description of the Gulf Stream." *Journal of Marine Research,* Vol. 40, Supplement, 1982.

Richardson, P. L., et al., "North Atlantic Subtropical Gyre: SOFAR Floats Tracked by Moored Listening Stations." *Science,* July 24, 1981.

Richardson, Philip L.:
"Benjamin Franklin and Timothy Folger's First Printed Chart of the Gulf Stream." *Science,* February 8, 1980.
"Gulf Stream Ring Trajectories." *Journal of Physical Oceanography,* January 1980.

The Ring Group, "Gulf Stream Cold-Core Rings: Their Physics, Chemistry, and Biology." *Science,* June 5, 1981.

Schuon, Marshall, "Vast, Swirling Rings Found to Be Vital to Gulf Stream's Complex Movements." *The New York Times,* August 19, 1980.

Sisson, Robert F., "Adrift on a Raft of Sargassum." *National Geographic,* February 1976.

Stuiver, Minze, Paul D. Quay and H. G. Ostlund, "Abyssal Water Carbon-14 Distribution and the Age of the World Oceans." *Science,* February 18, 1983.

Sullivan, Walter:
"Surface Ripples Found to Hide Huge Waves under Sea." *The New York Times,* August 12, 1980.
"Unseen World of Violent Storms Found on Ocean Bottom." *The New York Times,* September 21, 1982.

Vastano, Andrew C., and Philip L. Richardson, "Gulf Stream Cyclonic Rings." *Naval Research Reviews,* September 1976.

Webster, Bayard, "World's Oceans Became Cleaner Over the Last Decade, Study Finds." *The New York Times,* October 18, 1982.

Wehle, D.H.S., and Felicia C. Coleman, "Plastics at Sea." *Natural History,* February 1983.

Wiebe, Peter H., "Rings of the Gulf Stream." *Scientific American,* March 1982.

Wright, W. Redwood, "Currents of the Sea." *Natural History,* August/September, 1976.

Zahl, Paul A., "How the Sun Gives Life to the Sea." *National Geographic,* February 1961.

Other Publications

Cullen, Vicky, ed., *The Research Fleet.* The University-National Oceanographic Laboratory System.

FLIP: Floating Instrument Platform, 20th Anniversary, 1962-1982. Marine Physical Laboratory of the Scripps Institution of Oceanography, University of California, San Diego. MPL-U-30/82. June 1982.

Leppäranta, Matti:
"Modeling and Predicting Sea Ice Motion in the Baltic Sea." Institute of Marine Research, Helsinki, Finland. May 1980.
"On the Drift and Deformation of Sea Ice Fields in the Bothnian Bay." Research Report No. 29. Finnish Board of Navigation and Swedish Administration of Shipping and Navigation.

Martin, Roy E., ed., *Third National Technical Seminar on Mechanical Recovery & Utilization of Fish Flesh, Raleigh, North Carolina, December 1-3, 1980.* National Fisheries Institute, Washington, D.C.

National Marine Pollution Program Plan: Federal Plan for Ocean Pollution Research, Development, & Monitoring, Fiscal-Years 1981-1985, September 1981. Interagency Committee on Ocean Pollution, Research, Development, & Monitoring.

Schureman, Paul, *Tide and Current Glossary.* U.S. Department of Commerce, National Oceanic and Atmospheric Administration, National Ocean Survey. A Revision of U.S. Coast and Geodetic Survey Special Publication No. 228, 1949. Washington, D.C., 1975.

Whitemarsh, Lieutenant Commander R. P., "Great Sea Waves." *United States Naval Institute Proceedings, July 1934.* United States Naval Institute, Annapolis, Maryland.

The sources for the illustrations in this book are listed below. Credits from left to right are separated by semicolons; from top to bottom they are separated by dashes.

INDEX

Numerals in italics indicate an illustration of the subject mentioned.